"It is a great relief to know there is hope for me yet. This book is in my briefcase and I read it regularly – especially before shopping."

Vicki Gabereau
host, *Vicki Gabereau* show

"A timely and useful book for Boomers and others seriously interested in a comprehensive approach to financial planning for retirement."

David K. Foot
author, *Boom Bust & Echo*

"Diane is a welcome guest on my programs because she makes financial issues most of us find complex and confusing easy to understand."

Bill Good
CKNW radio talk show host and BCTV news anchor

"The attitude quiz alone is valuable. It not only helps you achieve a clear understanding about where you are and where you need to go financially – but personally too."

Jeff Dowle
Executive Vice President, HSBC Bank Canada, Vancouver

How Much Is
Enough?

How Much Is Enough?

Balancing Today's Needs with Tomorrow's Retirement Goals

Diane McCurdy, CFP

McGraw-Hill
Ryerson

Toronto Montréal Boston Burr Ridge, IL Dubuque, IA Madison, WI New York
San Francisco St. Louis Bangkok Bogotá Caracas Kuala Lumpur Lisbon
London Madrid Mexico City Milan New Delhi Santiago Seoul Singapore
Sydney Taipei

McGraw-Hill
Ryerson Limited
A Subsidiary of The McGraw-Hill Companies

ISBN: 0-07-088064-6

34567890 WEB 0987654321
Printed and bound in Canada.

Canadian Cataloguing in Publication Data

McCurdy, Diane (Lynn).
How much is enough? Balancing today's needs with tomorrow's retirement goals

Includes index.
ISBN 0-07-088064-6

1. Finance, Personal. 2. Retirement income – Planning. I. Title.

HG179.M3245 2000   332.024'01   C00-932814-9

Publisher: **Joan Homewood**
Editorial Co-ordinator: **Catherine Leek/Carrie Withers**
Production Co-ordinator: **Susanne Penny**
Editor: **Tita Zierer**
Electronic Page Composition/Line Art: **Sharon Lucas**
Cover Design: **Sharon Lucas**
Graphs Created By: **Don Pooley**
Cover Photo: **Donna Newman**

CONTENTS

Part Two: Getting Enough

PREFACE

Some people are musical, some can talk the birds out of the trees, some are born with the ability to make machines run. We all receive different God-given talents. Mine is handling money, and I'm very grateful for the gift.

When something comes so easily, it's easy to think that it's perfectly obvious to everyone else; but as a financial planner I've learned that's far from true. Over the years I've worked with many wonderful people for whom personal finance has been a mystery or a challenge, and they have taught me so much about the human side of money management. I learned early on that you can't just tell people what to do and have them go off and do it. You have to find the thing that motivates them to help themselves. And as I tried out different things on different people, I eventually developed the concept on which this book is based: everyone has a built-in emotional approach to money, and there are four of these fundamental attitudes.

My clients have also enlightened me on what people need to know and what they have trouble understanding—vitally important information for someone who wants to write a book that will help other people deal with their own financial lives.

I haven't always wanted to write this book. It evolved as I started to recognize that I could help people without being across a desk from them. The intent was to take away the mystery and perceived difficulty of managing money, and to share what I've learned from all those questions, quizzical looks and excuses that have come across the desk in my direction.

It's really important for me to feel that I can make a small contribution to improving the financial side of people's lives. I've never wanted any of my clients to feel that financial planning was all consuming. Rather, I want to make them feel they've taken care of it so it's a non-issue. With that out of the way, they have lots more room to live the other sides of their lives.

Financial concerns cause a great deal of anxiety, but worrying about them takes far more energy than just going ahead and taking care of them. I've tried to make this information so straightforward that it will no longer be a hurdle to get it done.

It would give me a great deal of pleasure if this book provides you with just one idea that makes you move forward to find financial peace of mind.

ACKNOWLEDGEMENTS

I believe that anything we ever accomplish, we don't accomplish alone; it's always in conjunction with others. And that belief is powerfully reinforced when one is writing a book. These are the particular others who helped me bring this book to life.

Paul Sullivan has been incredibly wonderful. Right from the beginning, three years ago, he kept me motivated and on the right track. Although he was in the throes of building his own business, Sullivan Media, he kindly gave his time and energy. His encouragement, direction and great editorial judgement made the book possible.

Elizabeth Wilson was able to capture and record all of the things I believed would be lost in the stream of half finished thoughts, enthusiasms and verbal meanderings. She did this all tirelessly and cheerfully. Elizabeth possesses a magic butterfly net that amazed me.

My colleague Don Pooley was a great resource, and gave some excellent additional suggestions. He's a man on the leading edge of technology.

Janice Bearg, of the Simon Fraser University Writing and Publishing Program, gave freely of her insight and expertise during the proposal stage.

Don Bedford, CGA, put a lot of effort into the toughest chapter.

Nobody could want a better friend or mentor than Ewen Stewart, who has believed in me from the start of my career. If everyone could have one person who believed in them like that in their lives they would be extremely fortunate.

Frank Harcourt taught me never to discount anything without looking at it first—one of the most important pieces of advice I have ever received.

Jack Newton and Howard Dawson also served as wonderful examples and helped me grow.

Betty Cooper is a great teacher.

My first banker, Ed Williams of the Toronto Dominion Bank, gave me my first loan back in the days when women couldn't get loans.

My two sisters, Heidy Black and Dorothy Walker put me to work when I was six. Today some people would call it child labour—they say they were teaching me entrepreneurial skills. I agree with them.

All my good friends made the road smoother. David and Doreen Godwin contributed in different ways. He had me and my office up to speed on computers in record time, otherwise I could never have finished the book. And she was a great sounding board for the ideas that ended up here. Another vote of confidence and encouragement came from my friends Sally and Michael Wright. Morning walks and talks with Anna Nyrady kept my head clear and allowed me to face whatever the day threw my way. Dorothy and George Petley are almost like second parents—the most wonderful, sweet people. Barbara Jones, Triss Bubbs, Ann Gagné, and Lesley Lerner are dear and supportive friends.

The office always runs smoothly because of Roberta Domae, Janet Marsh, and Michael Lee, with extra help from Mary Maciorowski, my best friend since childhood. They all make my life considerably easier through their fine work and engaging personalities. At the end when the book demanded so much of my time, my new partner David Mercier picked up the slack without a complaint. Thanks Dave.

At McGraw Hill, Joan Homewood and Julia Woods went to the mat to publish this book in record time. Their faith, and the calm efficiency of the other people who gave the book its final shape, spurred me on.

To all of my friends and family who don't seem to mind dealing with a total workaholic (I just think I'm enjoying myself). Thanks for being so patient.

And finally, Gordon Gutrath is a very special someone: constant, encouraging and full of love and support always. He's a gentle and generous soul who gives my life balance.

The greatest contributors to this book are my clients. I thank them from the bottom of my heart. It is because of them that I have been motivated to put together this program because the greatest satisfaction comes in helping people gain control of their financial lives by finding their enough number. I'm one of the fortunate few who has liked and enjoyed every client that has walked through the door. I thank you all!

INTRODUCTION

Enough—it's what we all want. But do you even know what enough is? For you, not for the facelift models on the tropical beach in the retirement commercial, or the guy down the street with a cappuccino machine in his BMW.

Nobody is typical. By discovering what you REALLY want, you can make sure you get it, now and in your retirement.

You're already asking, do I have to give something up? Yes. You have to give up not knowing where you are financially and being terrified that you'll run out of money. In exchange you'll gain control. You'll know what's important to you and you'll get it. You will know you have Enough. That's peace of mind.

How many times have I heard a client say, "Diane, I feel so good by the time I leave your office"? You'd think I ran a spa. But I'm a financial planner, and in my 26 years in this profession, I have seen thousands of clients smile with relief when they see their money working for them. It doesn't take long.

These are the same people who arrive at my office with sweaty palms and shifty eyes. Successful professionals—doctors, architects, media people, entrepreneurs—are embarrassed to admit that "I don't understand all that financial stuff," or "I'm so far behind I'll never catch up." If they're so successful in the rest of their lives, why are they no good at managing their money?

Their previous experience with financial planning or advice hasn't filled them with confidence, either. They complain that it all seems so all-consuming. To succeed, they feel pressure to alter their lives completely and start thinking and acting like Donald Trump, or at least Tony Robbins—totally driven to amass wealth the way ordinary people breathe.

Or, even worse, they get conned into believing that someone else will do it all for them. Someone else often has—losing a lot of their money, and handing them the bill. No wonder they're nervous.

Very few people have the ambition or the circumstances to achieve the exalted goals promised by so much financial advice. They end up feeling inadequate and giving up; falling back into their old habits—those that are familiar, at least. Money management ends up suffering the fate of all those other doomed resolutions, like losing 30 pounds, or quitting smoking.

So when people who walk into my office they often have an expectation that they're going to fail again. But at least they've decided it's time to do *something*. You too? What motivated you to pick up this book?

- Finances out of control?
- Don't know where it all goes?
- Doing OK, but not sure it's enough?
- Used to save more but can't find the money anymore?
- Confused about all the financial information out there?
- Started a lot of financial programs but never stayed on one?
- Slowing down and wanting to develop an exit plan?
- Want to get on track?
- Just beginning and want to do it right from the start?

Wherever you are now, whatever age or stage, I will give you the tools to get what you want and achieve financial freedom. Together we'll develop a unique, evolving program based on your situation and goals. And it won't just prepare you for retirement; it will reward you along the way.

PART ONE

If you're going to be successful, it won't be because everybody else thinks you are; it'll be because you've set your own goals and taken real, practical steps to make them happen. The wealthiest people aren't those who own the most stuff; they're the ones who manage their lifestyle best. This little idea works when so many big ideas fail.

You won't be doing anything extraordinary. You'll know who you are, what you want and how much you need to achieve it. You will be doing the right things regularly. That's it. It ain't sexy. It doesn't make good dinner party conversation ("I deposited $100 in my RRSP today. . ." Yawn.) But it works for client after client, time after time. In Part One I'll take you through four simple steps.

Your financial attitude

You have a built-in attitude toward money that controls the way you spend. It's as much a part of your outlook on the world as your sense of humour, and it doesn't change. With this program you'll find out what that attitude is. Once you've identified your type, you'll know where you're likeliest to run off the rails, and you'll gain some insight into why other people use money the way they do. This financial program has been designed to work with your financial attitude, rather than to try to change it.

Your cash flow

You'll keep track of everything you spend for at least a month. Does the thought of it send icy prickles down your spine? That's normal. But it's essential to find out where your money goes. Don't put it off waiting for a "typical" month. There's no such thing. And don't try to change your spending habits so that they live up to some imaginary standard. If you lie to yourself in this step, the others won't work. What is your salary, and how much of it do you keep? Can you reasonably expect it to go up or should you count on it staying the same? After you've finished, check what you spent against what you make.

Your assets and liabilities

You'll total up all of your assets: your RRSPs, savings, insurance policies, real estate and all investments. Then total your liabilities: mortgage, credit card bills, car payments, loans—anything you owe. Assets minus liabilities will give you your current net worth.

Your wish list

Besides a reliable retirement income, what do you want? A mint-condition 1956 Studebaker Golden Hawk? A year off in Micronesia? A wall-sized home theatre? A set of 400-threads-per-inch Egyptian cotton bedding? Make a wish list, and then sort it in order of priority. Don't judge yourself. This program is designed to make sure you have your luxuries along the way as you build up your retirement stockpile. Without those, you won't stick with the program, so these rewards are very personal choices.

In Chapter 4, you'll put all that information together and find your Enough Number. With a snapshot of your current financial status, you can project how much money you'll need to retire on and how much you need to save to get it. Looking at your cash flow, you can see how much you need to live on now and how much you can realistically put away each month. By comparing your cash flow to your wish list, you can see where your money is really going and compare that to where you want it to go. If you're fortunate enough that you have money left over, or you're already on a savings program, you'll know how much money you have to play with. If not, you'll have to sift though your spending to find the money you'll invest in yourself.

There. You've solved the number one financial challenge of your life. Your Enough Number will pay off doubly, because now that you have a plan, not only can you give yourself a comfortable retirement, you can enjoy peace of mind immediately.

That's the program. It will take you perhaps a day to get started, then an hour or so per month to maintain it. It has worked for all the people who have followed it and it will work for you. Even if you've left things too long, you'll be better off if you start now—and you'll feel better about your future.

PART TWO

In Part Two, you'll learn about how to get to your Enough number and work through the four key ways of getting there.

Start saving

Because you've kept track of your spending, you can see exactly where your money has been going. Somewhere in there is the answer to your question, "Where am I going to find the money to save?" When you know what you want, you can see what's keeping you from getting it and stop spending on things that don't mean as much to you. If you're in debt you'll probably have to deny yourself in the short term to achieve what you want in the longer term, but keep remembering, any money you spend in interest is money you can't spend on yourself.

Get financial advice

I strongly recommend that you get your own financial advisor because there are so many confusing options available now. A financial advisor can look at your entire financial picture and show you how to maximize your savings and investments in a way that doesn't keep you awake nights. Somewhere between Canada Savings Bonds and sowbelly futures, you'll find your comfort level. I'll also give you some general money-making strategies that will help your assets grow.

Invest wisely

It's so easy to get caught up in market trends and frenzies. But you can do better—and sleep better—investing for the long term. If that's entirely too boring for you, go ahead and use some of your extra on chasing The Next

Big Thing, but protect your principal. I'll show you how to balance your risk level—how much you crave or avoid risk—with your risk tolerance—how much risk your portfolio can stand.

Benefit from RRSPs and RESPs

Every year you can shelter 18% of your income from tax in an RRSP until you start using the money. That's a wonderful incentive to save, and the penalties for raiding your RRSP are so steep that it's a forced savings plan as well as a tax shelter. RESPs are a great way for parents to shelter after-tax money for their kids' education—and get a grant on top of it. I'll show you how you can get the greatest benefit from both of these programs.

Invest in yourself

If you're starting or running your own business, there's a chapter for you, with ideas for saving tax, splitting income and timing your saving program. Your own business can be one of the best investments you can make, so included in this chapter are some successful tactics for making your business grow. I'll cover estate planning for business owners as well.

Once you get there, then what? The final chapter deals with your own final chapter: how to get the most out of your retirement income and how to handle the money you want to leave behind. You need to set both in motion early, otherwise the government will take big bites.

Do you notice how time goes by faster and faster? Take control of your money now. If you don't, by the time you turn around, five years will have gone by. You'll wish you had.

Start your Enough program now and by the next time you wonder where the days and weeks went, compound interest will have worked its magic and you'll be pleasantly surprised at how your money has worked for you. Keep at it and on your next momentous birthday (39 again?), you'll be enjoying one or two of the items on your wish list. And when that morning comes that you don't have to get up and go to work, you'll know you have Enough.

Part 1

WHAT IS ENOUGH?

In over 26 years as a financial planner, I've learned one major fact about human behaviour: people don't change easily. They'll only change if they really want something.

CHAPTER

YOUR MONEY AND YOUR LIFE

I yam what I yam and that's all what I yam. — Popeye the Sailor Man

Money doesn't come cheap. It's wound up with our emotions in ways we seldom notice. We trade our time and energy for it, keep score with it, build with it, control others with it and indulge ourselves with it. Then we fantasize about having more. Some people's self-esteem rides on how much of it they have—or how much of it they can make others think they have. Some have trouble parting with it—if you spend it on something, it's no longer there helping you sleep at night! Some people believe they need money to buy the affection or respect of others. Others use it to protect themselves from pain, or to cause pain to others. People have lingering feelings of shame because as kids they had so much less, or more, than the others. There are those who consider themselves bad people if they care about money at all. Money is power. Money is glamour. Money is happiness . . .

I've got news for you. Money is just a tool. All that other stuff is what we put into it: fear, greed, envy, pride, anger, respect—that comes from us.

When Sue dragged Graham in to see me she was convinced that their finances were out of control. "How are we going to save any money when he keeps giving it all away?" she groaned. Neither she nor Graham had any idea how much they would need to retire on, so she wanted to put away every cent, just to be safe. As far as Graham was concerned, they had lots of money—certainly far more than either of them had grown up with—and as the son of a minister, he had always felt compelled to help others. That was why he had become a doctor. The money that went with the job gave his benevolent impulses new expression. As well as the charities and foreign foster children he supported, he had even been known to help out patients who were hard up.

Sue couldn't stand it. To her, having money meant just that: having it. She had grown up with even less than Graham, and she wanted to protect herself against ever being that poor again. After paying the monthly household expenses for a family of four with a mortgaged house, she wanted to save and invest anything that was left. Graham wanted to "give it all away." It became an ongoing tug-of-war that threatened to end their marriage.

That first visit from Sue and Graham brought home to me the two important points that underlie this book. First, only when you know how much is enough can you feel confident that you're on track and know what you have left to enjoy. Second, money is an emotional subject. People have deep-rooted attitudes about money, and their own attitudes have to be taken into account if any financial program is going to work for them. Let's start with the second point.

For Sue the only real security was money in the bank, and even with the pile of money that she had built up, she was anxious that it still wasn't enough. That nagging thought made her resent Graham for what she saw as lavishing money on strangers. But for him it seemed a shameful waste to have money sitting around in a bank account when any number of people and agencies were crying out for help.

When the two of them argued about money, neither realized that they were arguing about something far more profound than facts and figures. Neither one understood that the other's way of handling money reflected a deep emotional need, and to deny that need was to make the other feel insecure and unloved. When I met these two my first job was to help them understand that—and understand each other.

In my work I see four common attitudes toward money. None of them is right or wrong, better or worse than the others, but each can lead to trouble if it's not balanced. A person's ingrained attitude to money is not going to change, so it's essential to build a financial program around how each person feels about this pervasive fact of life. Let's begin by finding out what your attitude is. For each question in Figure 1.1, "The Attitude Quiz," write down the letter that most closely corresponds to your own point of view for each question. At the end you'll see what type you are, and where your personal pitfalls lie.

Figure 1.1: **The Attitude Quiz**

1. A) Shopping is my favourite sport.
   B) I shop when I need something.
   C) Shopping can be fun sometimes, especially if I'm shopping for other people.
   D) Shopping is torture.

2. A) Credit cards allow me to have what I want without worrying if I can afford it.
   B) If I can't afford something but it's an investment, why not use credit cards?
   C) I give my kids credit cards to teach them the value of money.
   D) Credit cards are a good way to build up a credit rating and a handy alternative to carrying cash.

3. When I go out for dinner with friends:

   A) We check out the latest hot restaurant, and we split the bill evenly.
   B) Sometimes I pay, sometimes they pay—it all works out eventually.
   C) I usually fight for the check.
   D) We ask for separate checks.

4. If I see something I like I:

   A) Buy it.
   B) Buy it if it fits into my game plan.
   C) Get one for me and one for somebody else if it's a good deal.
   D) Usually talk myself out of buying it.

5. If I won a big lottery I would:

   A) Never have to think about money again.
   B) Use it to create something important.
   C) Spend a lot of it on friends, family and charities, and keep enough to live on.
   D) Make sure my family was taken care of, pay off the mortgage, then live on the interest.

6. If I don't have any money in the bank I:

   A) Use my credit cards and line of credit — isn't that why they're there?
   B) Use credit to leverage opportunities.
   C) Worry that I won't be able to fulfill people's expectations of me.
   D) Get anxiety attacks (or I would if it ever happened).

7. A) I don't know where all my money goes.
   B) I always have a pretty good idea of how much money I have available, but never let that stand in the way of a good idea.
   C) Most of my money is allocated to family, charity or trying to make a difference.
   D) I keep close track of all my bank accounts and investments.

8. I love to use my money to:

   A) Enjoy life to the fullest.
   B) Follow my interests and stretch myself.
   C) Make other people happy.
   D) Build up a nest egg.

9. When I go shopping for something I need I:

   A) Usually come home with a few extras.
   B) Find it, buy it and go home.
   C) Look around to see if there's anything I can pick up for anyone else while I'm out.
   D) Shop around to make sure I'm getting it for the best price.

10. When I give to charity I:

    A) Give to the ones that appeal to my heart.
    B) Choose charities that most closely match my aims and beliefs.
    C) Give as much as I can because others need it more than I do.
    D) Allocate a specific amount to the charities of my choice.

11. A) It's important to get a new car every three years.
    B) If you buy the right car, it's a good investment.
    C) It's an incredible timesaver if everybody in the family has a car.
    D) I take really good care of my car to make it last.

12. When somebody has a new car I ask:

    A) Did it come loaded?
    B) What kind of car is it?
    C) Are you happy with it?
    D) How did it rate in Consumer Reports?

13. How do I choose my RRSP?

    A) What RRSP?
    B) My home/business/hobby is my retirement plan.
    C) My financial advisor takes care of all that.
    D) Carefully. Very carefully.

14. When I go on vacation I like to:

    A) Pamper myself.
    B) Get some use out of the trip.
    C) Take lots of friends or family with me.
    D) See how cheaply I can do it and still have fun.

HOW DID YOU SCORE?

What does money mean to you? It's helpful to know because any of these attitudes taken to the extreme can sabotage your dreams. Find out by adding up the As, Bs, Cs and Ds you have: the category in which you have the highest score is your type. You probably won't be one type exclusively, but one attitude will probably prevail. Once you know which type or combination of types you are, you'll have a better idea why you spend money in certain ways and you'll also be able to see patterns in your wish list, once you get to that part.

A) Spender

Motto: You only live once.

Dead giveaways: new car, latest gadgets, numerous garage sales to get rid of all the old stuff, credit card vacations

Spenders are very current. If you want something, ask one. They'll know where to get it, how to get it and probably the best deal on it. They're forward thinking, fun to be around, and often the envy of their friends. These are the fabled Joneses. If you walk into a house that has the best and the latest of everything, especially when the owners don't use it all, you're in a Spender's house. Spenders like money for the things it buys. They'd rather have something concrete than something abstract like savings. It doesn't have to be objects. It might be courses, or travel, or restaurant dining. They also tend to see shopping as a form of entertainment.

Danger zones: Spenders get into trouble when they spend everything they have—or more. Of the four types, they have the hardest time saving money. If you're a Spender and don't pay off your credit card bills every month, or have a permanent line-of-credit debt, you could be on the slippery slope.

Attitude adjustment: Once spenders buy into taking savings and expenses right off the top and having all the rest to spend, they're on their way.

Famous spender: Elton John. Most people, when asked how many Bentleys they own could make a pretty close estimate. Not Sir Elton. Maybe he doesn't know because he so seldom drives the things (at last count it was 14 or 15, for future reference). This man is probably the world's champion shopper. In one trip to Versace in Milan he spent $600,000. That was a leap even for him—$600,000 is usually the monthly total on his credit cards. But it wasn't his personal best. He's reputed to have spent $1.1 million in one day. Two truckloads of personal possessions accompany him everywhere he goes, no matter how short the trip. It's a good thing for him that the world's airwaves are clogged with oldies stations playing his songs and paying him a couple of cents in royalties every time they do, but even with that river of money coming to him, he once came within eight weeks of going broke.

B) Builder

Motto: Make it so.

Dead giveaways: midnight oil, own business, serious collection, big projects

For Builders, money is a tool. They use it—and sometimes risk it—to turn their plans and dreams into reality. The joy is in the creating. The self-made millionaire is the most obvious example of this type, but Builders might also work at mindless jobs and pour all their money and energy into restoring cars or painting watercolours. Most entrepreneurs, corporate leaders and ardent hobbyists are builders. These people make fantastic mentors (if they have the time). They may or may not have all the trappings of success, even if they can afford them.

Danger zones: Builders can get into trouble when they're so intent on building that they miscalculate the risks involved or fail to leave themselves a margin of error. The entrepreneur who keeps expanding the business without creating a cushion in case of failure, the collector who spends the mortgage money on a case of '82 Mouton Rothschild, the freelance consultant who buys a computer powerful enough to run the Navy and spends more time checking out what it can do than getting work—these are builders who could be headed for trouble. There can also be a tendency to start projects and not finish them. Often that leads to selling things at a loss, maybe from the last burning fascination, in order to get on with the Next Big Thing.

Attitude adjustment: Developing a portfolio is a building activity. Once Builders get interested in using their creativity here, they're on the escalator.

Famous builder: Bill Gates. In 1981 Bill Gates earned $1 million in personal income. But he was so busy with Microsoft that he didn't pay attention to his own bottom line. Whereas most people earning that kind of money have herds of accountants finding ways to shelter it, he was more interested in expanding his exploding company. He ended up writing a cheque for $500,000 in taxes. So rarely does this happen among the CEOs of America that he received a personal thank-you letter from Ronald Reagan.

C) Giver

Motto: 'Tis better to give than to receive.

Dead giveaways: mail from charities, well-dressed grandchildren, endless committee meetings

The rest of us probably couldn't get along without Givers. These are the volunteers, donors to charity and friends indeed. Givers feel good taking care of other people. They buy gifts for friends that they would never buy for themselves. They deny themselves so they can leave something for the children. They put time, energy and money into what they believe in. For some of them, having money is almost a sin, and the only proper thing to do with it is give it away. But for most, there's just a lot of pleasure in making other people happy or doing good.

Danger zones: Givers can get into trouble when they ignore their own needs. Tempting as it may be to help your kids buy their first homes, if you're doing it at the expense of your own retirement income, you could end up a burden to them in the long run. You might also be creating dependent children who never find out how to take care of money because there's always more where that came from.

Attitude adjustment: Once Givers understand that by taking care of themselves they're better able to take care of others, they'll happily get with the program.

Famous giver: Elvis Presley did not die a rich man—or at least not as rich a man as he should have been. He was famous for taking care of his family and his huge retinue of good old boys. All his famous spending sprees were for the benefit of others: building Graceland for his Mom and the rest of his kin, renting an amusement park for the night and taking all his friends, presenting Cadillacs to his buddies, buying a former presidential yacht and donating it to a children's hospital, contributing annually to 50 Memphis-area charities and buying a ranch near Memphis so he and his pals could go horseback riding. Not that there's anything wrong with that, but if he didn't really die, it's no wonder he's always spotted in 7-Elevens and laundromats.

D) Saver

Motto: A bird in the hand is worth two in the bush.

Dead giveaways: bag lunches, passbook bank accounts, Harvest Gold appliances

Without the Savers of this world, who would the rest borrow from? Savers can amass quite a lot and yet still have an enviable quality of life on a tiny salary. Or they can just get to wherever everybody else wants to be sooner than everybody else. Other types can't quite figure out how they do it. Savers are very good at spotting money-wasting activities and avoiding them—some to the point that other people consider them cheap. These are not impulsive people, and they're often very organized. They'll ask those difficult questions like "How are you going to pay it back?" Savers can have a bit of trouble parting with their money. Some are good investors, but some don't want to risk anything and prefer cash. For peace of mind they need savings as a cushion.

Danger zones: Savers can be too conservative with their investments so their money doesn't grow as much as it could. And they sometimes postpone enjoying their money until it's too late and they can't do the things they've always wanted.

Attitude adjustment: Once Savers have their Enough number and know that they can meet their security needs while still enjoying themselves along the way, they start to feel a bit freer about spending.

Famous Saver: Hetty Green, the Witch of Wall Street. Hetty, who lived from 1834 to 1916, inherited several million dollars at age 21. Her financial genius turned her fortune into what today would be $17.3 billion, which places her among the 40 richest people in the history of the U.S. Spending it was another matter. When the hem of her long dress became dirty, she would go to the laundry, ask that they "wash only the bottom" and wait in her bloomers until her dress was cleaned. She is said to have spent hours looking for a two-cent stamp she had lost. When she was a kid, she refused to have the candles on her birthday cake lit. Next day she cleaned them off and returned them for a refund.

Combinations

Most people find that they are combination types. If your top two choices were about equal, here are the combination pitfalls you should watch out for.

SPENDER-BUILDER

The big danger is overextending the business or pouring money that they don't have into the hobby. Spender-Builders need to make sure they create a cushion so they can take it to the edge and not fall off.

SPENDER-GIVER

The temptation to spend *and* to give away money can leave the Spender-Giver with a warm feeling inside but living in a cold-water flat. An off-the-top savings program is imperative.

SPENDER-SAVER

Seems like an unlikely combination, but these are the people who make sacrifices to save because they know they should, then they want something and blow all their savings because they "deserve it." They lose the compounding effect of their savings and have to start again from scratch. It would have been better to save less, consistently, and reward themselves occasionally, than to feel that they're straitjacketed and have to break loose.

BUILDER-GIVER

These good-hearted folks are wonderful if they build first and share later. Some of the greatest philanthropists are this type. But if they don't do it in the right order they can undermine themselves in many ways: building a successful enterprise of some sort then giving it all away, ignoring their own project to help someone else who's in trouble, or devoting so much volunteer time and energy that they're not providing for themselves or their family. They need to make providing for their own needs a priority.

BUILDER-SAVER

Builder-Savers can sabotage their own efforts by being too cheap and not investing in things that would make their lives easier or help their businesses grow. They sometimes don't value their own time enough and end up doing things the hard way. That isn't really saving. But if everything is in balance, this type can go far.

GIVER-SAVER

These people give, but with strings attached. This can work when the strings will help the receivers understand the value of the gift (like offering to help the kids with a down payment on the condition that they save an equal amount) but in extreme cases Giver-Savers run into emotional blackmail. Some feel they won't be loved if they don't give when "asked," so they're constantly at war with themselves. Others use money as a bludgeon to control their nearest and dearest—"do what I say or I'll write you out of the will." It's hard to be happy under those circumstances.

TWO ATTITUDES, ONE FAMILY

In a recent survey of 700 marriage counselors, money was listed as sixth among the major causes of breakup. (Communication breakdown came first—and I'm willing to bet that arguments about money caused a lot of *that.*) When two people who live together don't respect each other's attitudes, there's bound to be trouble, as you saw with Graham and Sue. "I'm right, you're wrong." "You don't love me."

Some conflicts come and go like visiting in-laws. Money is with us all day, every day, and our own attitudes are so deeply embedded that we don't even know we have them. A different one can seem just plain wrong.

At that point we have two immovable positions and one constant irritant. Not exactly the basis of an intimate, loving relationship.

Is compromise possible? It is, but only if each person understands how the other feels about money and is willing to respect it. When we're arguing about money, we honestly think we're talking simple facts and figures, but we're not. Even though we're dealing with columns of numbers, this is not a rational subject; it's a deeply emotional one. Understanding that goes a long way to finding a middle ground. Attitudes are not right or wrong, and they tend not to change.

The only way to compromise is to acknowledge the other person's needs and create a budget that will allow both people to have some of what they need. With Graham and Sue, once they had their Enough number, Sue knew exactly how much she needed to save, so she felt more secure about allowing Graham to indulge his need to help other people. They settled on an amount that he could donate each month without disrupting the family finances. Best of all, the money arguments stopped and their relationship improved immensely.

In future chapters, you'll learn about setting goals and managing your money so that you can reach them. For now, make a start on acknowledging that neither of you is right or wrong, and each of you has certain emotional-financial needs that must be fulfilled before you both can feel comfortable.

ATTITUDES VS. PREFERENCES

Keep in mind that our attitudes control *how* we like to spend our money. Preferences are a different matter. These determine *what* we spend our money on, and though opposing preferences can cause a lot of conflict, they don't go as deep emotionally as attitudes, so they're easier to deal with. Jack and Jill might both be Spenders (attitude) but he would spend all their money on landscaping and she'd rather spend it all on golfing (preferences).

When I work with them, I'll first make sure they're not spending everything they have, because two people with the same attitude can egg each other on and take that attitude to the extreme. Only when we've figured out how much they need to save and started a saving program will we start dealing with how much goes to landscaping and how much goes to golf. For this initial discussion, stick to attitudes and try to keep preferences out of it. We will deal with those later.

MONEY MYTHS

Attitudes may be with us for life, but there are some wrongheaded ideas out there that should be discarded. These are myths that we cling to because they offer some hope or give us an excuse for doing nothing.

Myth 1: "I'm going to inherit."

Sure. And what if your parents live to 110? Or what if they haven't set up their affairs properly and most of your inheritance goes to fees and taxes? Even if you believe you're going to inherit something, don't count on it, and don't include your great expectations when you calculate your assets.

Myth 2: "There's always Canada Pension."

Forget the scare stories that CPP won't even be there by the time you need it—even if it is, the maximum monthly pension cheque is only about $900, certainly not enough to live on.

Myth 3: "Why bother saving? The government just takes it all anyway."

Nobody is crazy about paying taxes. But the government has given you a way to save money AND save taxes. Every dollar you put into your RRSP and leave there until you retire is a dollar you can deduct from your income tax now. Something is better than nothing, so if you haven't been using your RRSPs, start now.

Myth 4: "I was born poor; I'll always be poor" or – "I was born rich; I'll always be rich."

Both rich and poor can use money management skills—the poor to grow richer and the rich to keep from becoming poor. Even if you've never had much money and you don't make much, you can tend it carefully and make it grow. And if you grew up rolling in it, learn not to take it for granted.

Myth 5: "I'll be fine as soon as: I marry rich; I win the lottery; my ship comes in."

Hey, you never know. But statistically you have a pretty good idea. Just to be on the safe side, assume that no one's going to take care of you but you.

Myth 6: "Mutual funds will make me rich."

Successful mutual funds will probably outperform guaranteed savings, like bonds or GICs, but not enough to make you wildly rich. Remember too that they carry some risk, and they can go down. Lots of inexperienced investors get panicky when that happens. Mutual funds can also come with fees for buying or selling, and those have to be taken into account. The price of mutual funds fluctuates with the number of people buying, so most people tend to buy them high around RRSP time.

Myth 7: "This deal guarantees that I'll get a 60% return on my investment in a year."

If it sounds too good to be true, it is. There's a reason that's an old saying. No deal can guarantee you huge returns without huge risks. The people who are trying to get your money have put a lot of time and effort into making their deal seem sweet as pie, but they're likely to leave you with the soggy crust.

Myth 8: "Everyone's doing better than I am."

The people with the yacht could well be in debt up to their eyeballs. And the ones who got in on Gaspex.com when it was 13¢ and now it's $86 are probably talking about a very small part of their portfolio. You can bet they don't pepper their dinner party conversation with the stories of Doofus Industries, which sank like a stone, taking thousands of their dollars with it.

Myth 9: "I'll never get old."

Consider the alternative.

So, having considered the alternative, you're starting to think that maybe you *will* be looking at retirement someday. Will it be a time of comfort and enjoyment, or will you spend your golden years worrying that you'll run out? In the next chapter, you'll take the first concrete steps toward a no-worry retirement.

CHAPTER

WHERE IT GOES

To be satisfied with what one has; that is wealth. As long as one sorely needs a certain additional amount, that man isn't rich. — Mark Twain

Before we look into the future we need an unobstructed view of right now. How much do you have? What do you owe? Where does your money go? You'll answer those vital questions over the next couple of months.

There are two main parts to this project: *tracking your cash flow* and *calculating your net worth.* If you panic at the thought of it, you're not alone. A lot of people "manage" their finances by shutting their eyes and believing that somehow everything will work out all right. If that's not good enough for you anymore, grit your teeth, brace yourself and get ready to look your finances in the face. Spenders, Givers and Builders, you need to trust this process. Maybe it scares you to death right this minute, but this is your first step toward peace of mind in the future. You'll have to focus more on your spending behaviour temporarily to discover your Enough number, but through this short-term-pain exercise you'll be able to spend, give or build more effectively down the road.

TRACKING YOUR CASH FLOW

Next to "how much is enough?" "where does it all go?" has to be the question I hear most often. That question is actually quite simple to answer. In fact it has to be answered if you're going to get control of your money and your future. Here's what you do: keep track of every cent you spend over the next month, or, preferably, two months. Every single cent.

I know this isn't a good month to start. The car insurance is due; the bills from your vacation are in; you have to buy school supplies; you're holding a family reunion; it's Chinese New Year; you paid your brother's bail and he skipped . . . No, it's nothing at all like all those *typical* months where nothing ever happens and no unexpected expenses pop up. Maybe you should wait for one of those.

No month is typical. Start now.

Keeping Track

Keeping track of every cent you spend is an adjustment, so it's important that you find a way that's convenient and comfortable for you. Here are some methods that have worked for my clients:

- Carry around a little notebook and record each expenditure when you make it.
- If you've got an electronic planner, enter everything into one file and later download it into your computer.
- If you carry one of those mini-tape recorders, record each purchase as you make it.
- Get a receipt for everything and put them all in a file folder or envelope that you carry around. (Don't just shove them in your pocket or purse.) For those times when you don't get a receipt, write the date, purchase and cost on the file folder or envelope.

At home you'll want to keep a master record. At the end of each month you'll categorize your purchases, add up the total for each category and also total the categories. You should keep this record out in the open somewhere so it reminds you to write everything down when you come home. It might look like Figure 2.1, "A Sample Record of Expenses."

If you prefer, you can keep your master record on computer, as long as that's what's easiest. There are a lot of personal finance software programs available that have a cash flow feature. These programs conveniently break your expenses down into categories.

Here are some things to keep in mind when you're making your master record.

- Keep a record for each person who's spending the household income. That way you'll have a more accurate account of where the money is going.

Figure 2.1:   **A Sample Record of Expenses**

Thomas			Brenda		
Apr.1	$1450.00	mortgage	Apr.1	$343.22	utilities
	$37.50	groceries			
	$26.31	hardware	Apr.2	$11.16	groceries
	$4.74	coffee		$18.34	books
	$79.84	tires		$58.30	medicine
				$22.41	personal supplies
Apr.2	$6.36	coffee & muffin		$2.52	juice
	$7.32	lunch			
			Apr.3	$4.25	coffee
Apr.3	$27.50	bus tickets		$3.77	lunch
	$1.35	newspaper		$10.00	baby gift

- Record every expenditure, even the little things. They add up.
- Account for each purchase separately: $652 for the Visa bill doesn't tell you anything.
- Decide at the beginning whether you're going to write down credit card purchases when you make them or copy them down from the itemized bill; otherwise you might duplicate some items.
- Record your purchases in your master record every day, while they're still fresh in your mind. It takes only a couple of minutes, and that way if you forgot to write something down you'll recollect it.
- If you're self-employed and not incorporated, record everything. If you're incorporated, write down only your personal expenses.
- Total everything up at month's end so you'll have separate totals for each month.
- If you forget for a few days, start over. You need a continuous record of your spending, not one with gaps. A lot of my clients have had to start over two or three times. Don't worry. Once you get into the habit, it becomes easy to keep track. Some of my clients, generally Savers and Builders, have found this so useful that they do it all the time, but that's a personal choice.

I know this sounds like a lot of trouble, but it really doesn't take that much time if you're systematic, and you will reap some wonderful rewards from it almost instantly. Don't give up. It'll be worth the trouble, I promise.

CASH FLOW STATEMENT

At the end of each month, it's time to add up the numbers. Now this is the part that stops some people dead. They've faithfully written down every expenditure for weeks. Now those columns of numbers look seriously imposing, and if they don't total them, somehow they won't have to know the awful truth.

No matter how many times I ask people to add up their lists before they bring them in, 90% of them don't. Then I have to do it, and they end up paying me to add numbers—something they could have done themselves for free—so I understand what a psychological hurdle this is. Remember, it's just a snapshot. You can make this step a little more fun by estimating the totals before you do the math, or even before you start keeping track. You'll probably find you're way off in some areas.

Before you get out your calculator, arrange your purchases by category in Figure 2.2, "Cash Flow Statement." This form, which can also be downloaded from **www.how-much-is-enough.com**, covers everything. It will help you remember annual and occasional expenses that you may not have covered during the months that you were keeping track. For annual expenditures, divide the annual amount by 12 and enter that figure for the month. If it's an occasional expense like home and property maintenance, where you might have to paint every 10 years, replace the roof or maybe put in a new furnace, look at your records and try to come up with a yearly average. Divide that by 12 for your monthly record.

Once you've calculated your total expenditures, subtract them from your monthly income. If your income is irregular or hard to predict, take a monthly average.

If you are living within your means but still having trouble finding money to save, the Figure 2.2, Cash Flow Statement will show you where it's hiding. You'll be able to see where you're spending on things that don't mean that much to you, and how much you can save by cutting back on them. For example, I know some very busy people who once belonged to book clubs but had no time to read books. When they realized how much they were spending on hardcovers they never read, they were a bit shocked. There were other places where they would rather have spent that money. Some even chose to save it.

If you're spending more than you're earning, your Cash Flow Statement will tell you why. You might have had an unusual month and there was a big expense that you don't usually have to deal with.

Figure 2.2: **Cash Flow Statement**

Category	Person 1	Person 2
Home		
Mortgage, rent or maintenance fees		
Home & property maintenance		
Property tax		
Property insurance		
Heating, electricity, water/sewer		
Household Expenses		
Food (dining out goes under Entertainment in Miscellaneous)		
Lunches		
Telephone		
Computer, internet service and cable		
Newspapers & magazines		
General household supplies		
Furnishings, equipment & appliances		
Loans & Credit Cards		
Credit card payments on outstanding balance		
Loan payments other than mortgage and car		
Personal		
Clothing		
Laundry & dry cleaning		
Life and disability insurance		
Toiletries		

Category	Person 1	Person 2
Medical		
Provincial plan		
Prescription and non-prescription drugs		
Dentist		
Optician & glasses		
Other treatments		
Transportation		
Car payments		
Insurance/licence		
Car maintenance		
Parking, bus, subway		
Miscellaneous		
Club fees		
Entertainment		
Vacations/vacation home		
Special occasions: birthdays, holidays		
Donations and gifts		
Children's allowances, lessons, sports		
Education		
Income tax (if not deducted from wages)		
RRSPs		
Other savings & investment money		
Other expenses		
Monthly Income Per Person:		
Total Expenditures Per Person:		

That's okay if you're living within your means and the expense will be covered in a month or two. But if "unusual" expenses crop up all the time, and they're piling up, you're cutting it too close. You're regularly spending more than you make if you carry credit card or line-of-credit debt all the time and this month's big bill put you even further in the glue. Your Cash Flow Statement will show where the money needs to go versus where it's going now. Knowledge is power.

CALCULATING THE FUTURE

Much can change between now and when you retire. Our lives are not fixed. Priorities shift. Children do unexpected things. The economy can take unpredictable turns. Still, there are a few changes that we can predict, so we might as well take them into account in the calculations for your Enough number. Check the circumstances that will apply to you at retirement age, then write down the amount that can be taken off your monthly expenses in Figure 2.3, "When I Retire..."

You'll note that there's no entry line for Selling the House and Moving to a Cheaper Place. I don't include the value of your home in this calculation. In my experience, most people stay put, despite their intentions to trade down. They start looking at condominiums or smaller houses and realize that they'd have to give up too much to trade down. If they do trade down, by the time the transaction costs are calculated in, there doesn't appear to be a huge saving, even if they do gain something in simplicity. Or they make a trial move to a prettier/cheaper/warmer region and

Figure 2.3: **When I Retire...**

	Person 1: Reduction to Monthly Expenses	Person 2: Reduction to Monthly Expenses
Mortgage will be paid off.		
Children's education paid for.		
Children will live on their own.		
Will only need one car.		
No more insurance premiums.		
No pension or RRSP contributions		
Other		
Total		

find they miss their community. Such decisions have to wait until the time comes, so we can't include them in the calculations. But reaching your Enough number will at least give you the freedom to choose.

Subtract this total from your current Total Expenditures per Person, the last line in Figure 2.2, Cash Flow Statement and put the sum in the box below. If you retired now, this number is how much you would need per month to live on this year. By adjusting this figure for inflation, we'll determine how much you'll need to live on when you do retire.

Total Expenditures Per Person After Retirement:		

Congratulations. You've completed the hardest part of the program. Although there are a few more tasks to do before we can determine your Enough number, none of them takes more than an hour or two. Just looking at your Cash Flow Statement can give you a pretty clear idea of where you stand, even without doing the rest. But keep going anyway, to get the whole picture.

PERSONAL BALANCE SHEET

Your net worth is what you have minus what you owe—assets minus liabilities—simple as that. It's another starting point to finding your Enough number, and it's the annual tally that shows how close you are to reaching that number. It might even tell you you're there already. Fill in Figure 2.4, "Personal Balance Sheet — Assets" and Figure 2.5, "Personal Balance Sheet — Liabilities" now, and go through it every year to check your progress. I love doing this once a year to see how, as I contribute, my money is making money on its own.

I've left out personal effects like furnishings, art, jewelry and other collectibles because most people don't sell those things unless they're desperate. If you have been collecting these things as an investment and intend to sell them, put them under "Other assets." I've also left out future inheritances. Once you inherit you can claim the assets, but until you do, they're somebody else's.

By doing your Cash Flow Statement and Personal Balance Sheet, you've accomplished three things. First, you've started paying attention. That's half the battle. Second, you've organized all your financial papers— and how long have you been intending to get around to *that?* Finally, you've gathered the main figures we'll use in Chapter 4 to calculate your

Figure 2.4:   **Personal Balance Sheet — Assets**

Assets	Person 1	Person 2	Joint
Liquid			
Cash			
Canada Savings Bonds			
Life insurance cash values			
Guaranteed Investment Certificates			
Short term deposits			
Other			
Total Liquid Assets			
Semi-liquid			
Total personal RRSP			
Group RRSPs through employment			
Non RRSP			
Bonds, preferred shares			
Mutual funds, common stock			
Investment real estate			
Mortgages			
Annuities			
Bonus plans			
Income averaging annuities			
Other			
Total Semi-liquid Assets			
Fixed (current total values)			
Residence			
Seasonal residence			
Business interest/professional practice			
Other assets			
Total Fixed Assets			
Total Assets			

Figure 2.5: **Personal Balance Sheet — Liabilities**

Liabilities	Person 1	Person 2	Joint
Outstanding loans, line of credit			
Loans against life insurance			
Credit card outstanding balance			
Remaining mortgage(s)			
Income tax owed			
Other			
Total Liabilities			
Net Worth			

Enough number and how to reach it. If you're a Spender, Builder or Giver you can tell even now if you're out of control. If you're a Saver, you'll probably get the warm fuzzies just looking at what you've done so far, but don't get too smug. Eventually, you might have to do a bit of behaviour modification too.

In either case, now the hard work is behind you. You deserve a rest. Relax and indulge in a little fantasy. You're on your way to Enough and the next step is to decide how you'll reward yourself.

CHAPTER

WHAT YOU WANT

There is nothing like a dream to create the future. — Victor Hugo

How much is enough? Enough for what?

The whole point of this program is to give you the tools to get what you want. But do you know what you want? Have you sat down and made a list, or is it all just jostling around somewhere in the back of your mind? "Gee, someday I'd love to…" Your wants, needs and goals are unique to you, and they're a vital factor in calculating your Enough number.

Chapter 2 gave you an accurate picture of how much you're spending and how much you're taking in. Now that you've kept track of your spending for a month (preferably more) you've probably had a few surprises. I can't tell you how often I've heard "I never realized how much it costs to live!" or "I had no idea where my money was going!" It's so easy just to drift along, covering your expenses and spending when you think you need something, but now you can see the consequences.

Are things going exactly as you want them to go? Stop drifting. You can only get to where you're going if you know where that is. Time to draw yourself a map.

WHAT *DO* YOU WANT, ANYWAY?

If you know what you want, you can get it. If you don't, there's no chance. In this chapter, I'll show you how to set yearly goals and decide how you're going to reward yourself as you save for retirement. These discovery exercises will help you look beyond your immediate temptations and determine if there is balance and meaning in your life, financially and otherwise. Then you can begin to make the changes you need to—and you'll be motivated to stick with them.

We're all seduced and sidetracked by different things. Builders often get so caught up in the process of building that they don't profit from their labours. They become fascinated with something new and just want to move on, or they run short of cash, then sell their current project for less than it's worth. Now they don't have enough for their next project and they become frantic about their resources. A lot of Builders spend their lives overextended. If that sounds eerily familiar, these exercises will help you clarify what you're after and stick to thing number one so that you can go on to thing number two with an easy mind. As one Builder told me, "The first time you learn how to make it; the next time you learn how to keep it."

Savers take joy in the act of saving: of watching the numbers add up and compound. What most of them don't like to do is spend, even when they can afford to. If you've been trading pleasure for a hefty bank account, you may have a little trouble making a wish list, but that's exactly why you should do it. It's the first step to rewarding yourself for all that self-denial. Remember, all Savers become givers eventually. Wouldn't you rather get a little fun out of that money yourself than have it all go to someone else when you're gone?

Self-denial is certainly not a Spender's big problem. I've seen so many of them wasting a lot of their money, or worse, borrowing somebody else's, in the name of instant gratification. Are they using and enjoying the things they have, or does much of their stuff end up in the backs of closets or taking up room in the basement? Are they letting advertisers and salespeople tell them how to spend their money—the money they sacrifice their time and leisure for?

If you're a Spender, decide what you truly want; then you can get it rather than being constantly deflected by the siren song of More Stuff—and you can get it without feeling that you're depriving yourself. If you can't live without impulse shopping, you can have that too. Anything that's important to your sense of contentment is part of the calculation.

For a Giver, the biggest spur is someone else's need, real or perceived. But in taking care of the rest of the world, they often fail to recognize that they have goals and desires too. In fact, the very thought of putting themselves first may go against the grain. If you'd rather give than receive, these exercises will give you a reason to examine some of your own desires that you've been ignoring. You need to learn that taking care of yourself is an important part of taking care of others. Your wish list and goals can include giving to others, but they also need to include giving to you.

Are you ready to take control? Start by making two lists every year. The first should be a wish list of things you want to acquire. The other is a list of your personal, career, financial and relationship goals. Throughout the year, these two lists will remind you what you're after and motivate you to get it.

WISH LIST

Enjoying your money now is just as important as having enough later. Your wish list is the list of treats that you will reward yourself with as you save for retirement. Here's a chance to think about the things you spend money on, or want to spend money on, and decide which ones are truly important to you. Don't judge yourself. If it's something you really want, it goes on the list, even if somebody else might think it's bad or outrageous or self-indulgent. Self-indulgence is what your wish list is all about. (Did you hear that, Givers?)

Your wish list should include rewards that are specific to your type. If you're a Spender, it's a good idea to include a couple of unspecified shopping sprees with specified spending limits. For you, shopping itself is fun, and you'd be frustrated if you couldn't go on a mall rampage every now and then. If you're a Giver, figure out how much you want to give each year and put that in your wish list.

Figure 2.2, the Cash Flow Statement that you've recorded for over a month (preferably two or more), will be a big help here, because sometimes we don't even realize how important something is to us until we see how much money we spend on it. You might notice that you're spending $40 a week on CDs and think that's money you could save. If you buy them, listen once and then never play them again, it certainly is. But if you get a lot of enjoyment out of that music and would feel deprived without it, why mess around? The CDs might as well be part of your reward. Examine your cash flow statement for those surprise rewards.

Practical things belong on your wish list too, like a new car or new carpeting for the house—big expenditures that don't come along often that you would have to save up for.

And, finally, the wish list is a place for your dreams: the boat, the antiques, the six months travelling around India. Sometimes these items also appear on your list of yearly goals. These are the things that you've always said you want, but never truly thought you could get. You can. Maybe not this year or next, but eventually.

Another important part of this exercise is to write down what each wish will cost. It might require a bit of research to find out, but once you have a figure, you can aim for it. You can also decide on your priorities once you see the costs stacked up against each other: if you spend $100 less on clothes per month, you can take that trip to the Turks and Caicos a year sooner—*and* own your own diving equipment.

Remember that if you save for something and pay no interest, it costs you less. Instead of giving somebody else your money (for nothing), you can be using it all to get the things that you want most. The interest you don't pay the bank goes toward buying your next treat.

WISH LIST TIMES TWO

It's easier to make a list when you're single, because you've only got to think about yourself. But when you are part of two (or more), you have to incorporate someone else's wishes into your life, and here's where it gets complicated. This is where fights can start. Here's a source of divorce.

Make your wish lists separately. I can't emphasize this enough. It's too easy for one person to dominate the process if you try to do it together. The objective is to discover what each of you wants, without being judgmental. Who knows? You might even find out some things about each other that you didn't know before.

Quite often couples will have a lot of the same things on their lists— which is maybe why they're together in the first place. For items in common, it's just a matter of making priorities. Get together and look at those you both want and decide on an order for achieving them. Usually the expensive items go to the bottom of the list and people save for them while they enjoy some of the less expensive ones.

Things can get tricky when a couple's wish lists have a lot of differences. Generally up to this point, one person has been more persuasive or demanding, and the other, who gives in all the time, is stewing in resentment: "You always get your way and I never get mine." Now's the time to start playing fair.

I've heard too many sad stories about people who broke up because the one who made more money felt entitled to more say in how it was spent. In one nightmare marriage, the husband—we'll call him Bob—kept all his income for himself. He bought workshop tools, he bought a luxury car, he went on fishing and golfing expeditions with his pals. In the meantime, the wife—we'll call her Susie—was expected to buy all the food, pay the mortgage and buy the kids' clothes and school supplies out of her income. When Bob took out a second mortgage on the house, without consulting Susie, to spend on "investments," that was the last straw. She realized that he was never going to change, and in the not unlikely event that he went down, he'd take her with him. Once they separated, she realized that she was too much of a Giver and he was too much of a Spender and they had never addressed that problem. She belatedly understood how the sheer tension of the financial situation had been tearing her apart and making the kids miserable too. Susie's starting over.

Pool Your Resources

Fair isn't always equal. It's not like a business, where the auditor comes in at the end of the year to account for every penny or every hour spent. Fair means that you both have an equal share in the family lifestyle, no matter who makes what. But you should also both have private money to spend as you like.

If you're a couple, you're a couple. You both contribute in innumerable ways, and money is only one of them. Some couples prefer to keep their money jointly and others keep their money separate and work out ways to divide expenses. Either way is fine, and it's important not to have such hard and fast rules that people feel straitjacketed. But both of you have to feel that you're being treated fairly or there will be what are ever-so-gently called "issues."

The only rule is to take care of your needs first: household expenses, food, retirement savings, elimination of debt. You might not have a lot of financial resources because you've made the decision that one of you is going to take a less stressful job in order to take care of the kids. In that case I recommend pooling all your money, then allocating it. If you're both working and there's more money, you might want to keep a certain amount of your own income separate after you've jointly taken care of expenses. With some couples who have lots of money, neither person is even aware what the other is spending money on. As long as you're taking care of your immediate needs and your financial future, then who cares?

Something that works in both cases is to keep a common bank account for food, household expenses and anything else you share equally. You might also want to contribute to a common savings account for your bigger wish list items.

Split the Pocket Money

I suggest that you allocate two separate allowances, one for each of you, for little things. Each should have the same amount of private discretionary money, regardless of any difference in incomes, and it doesn't matter what the other person spends that money on.

Take Turns

If you can't afford to take care of two wish lists at the same time, alternate. Toss a coin if you have to, to see who goes first, and then fulfill items on your wish lists one after the other. Jack can have his new computer and Jill can rebuild the back stairs without coming to loggerheads. If there's no common goal to work on first, start off with a few of the less expensive items and try to save for the more expensive ones at the same time.

Work Together

If you're involved in a common project, a good way to avoid arguments is to agree that you both have to love it before you'll buy it. A client told me that this worked like magic for her and her husband when they were building their house, even though she was the first one to have to give up something she loved. She found that with every element that one of them had to give up, the final compromise turned out to be something better.

Respect Each Other

Finally, remember what you learned about yourselves in Figure 1.1, The Attitude Quiz. You can't change each other, so if your other half would qualify for the Olympic power-shopping team and you're a Saver who's not happy unless you put money in a GIC every month, accept each other's financial differences, difficult as that may be. Oddly enough, it's the little things that cause the most upsets. "I don't want anything for myself! I want to upgrade this house so we'll get more money for it when we sell it. All you want is to waste money going on trips!" As long as you're living within your means and on track for retirement, you both have a right to financial self-expression. You get separate money to do with as you wish. You are different people with different needs. Neither of you is right and neither of you is wrong. Breathe deeply and repeat.

Remember that you are a family and you chose to be together, so always be respectful when you're going through this process. There will be tradeoffs. If you work out a system that's fair, both of you will feel that your needs are being met and a lot of the old money issues will simply disappear.

WISH LIST FAVOURITES

Wish list items aren't restricted to what can be accomplished in a year, although you should review them yearly. Here are some of the most common wishes.

Children's Education

This is a big priority for a lot of parents, and it's nice to know that RESPs can offer some tax relief while you save for the kids' university, college or technical school. They work like RRSPs, in that you can invest the money any way you like, so if you're a smart investor your RESPs can probably outperform any savings account on Earth. I'll talk more about RESPs in Chapter 8. Private schooling, various kinds of specialized lessons and coaching also require a bit of planning, so they go on the wish list too.

Early Retirement

Another big one. Retirement is probably why you bought this book, and if you're working through the exercises, you'll soon know when you can retire and on how much. Don't forget also that retirement is a huge change in your life and it requires emotional preparation as well as financial.

Renovations

Some renovations, like adding a swimming pool, make your home more enjoyable without necessarily increasing its value. Others—a kitchen upgrade, for instance—will increase your enjoyment of your home and you'll get some or all of the investment back when you sell the house. In either case, renovations tend to make life miserable while they're underway, so don't add financial stress to the whole ordeal. Save up.

First Home

If you pay rent for 25 years, you're buying *somebody* a house. Might as well be you. Buying your first home is almost always a solid investment. I say that advisedly. In Vancouver, where I live, we had a plague of leaking condominiums that cost the owners thousands of dollars each to fix. Many people, already stretched to the limit, could do nothing but walk away. Do your research, try to wait for a buyers' market and don't mortgage yourself to the hilt.

Upgrading to a New Home

As family needs change, this often becomes a priority. Moving up to a better home is something to think about when you've built a good pile of equity in your current one. It's especially worthwhile if your mortgage payments will stay the same or go down in proportion to what you make. If you're looking at a much higher percentage of your income going into the mortgage, ask yourself, do you really want to be house-poor again?

Vacations

It's essential, no matter how poor you are, to take a break, even if it's Sunday afternoon in the park. So although the class and duration of your vacation depends on your financial capacity, most people recognize the need to recharge their batteries. If the long or expensive trip you dream about seems beyond your reach, put it on your list anyway. You can start saving now.

Vacation Home

Only rarely are these an investment—at least financially. For many families, though, that doesn't matter. The vacation home is where tensions fall away and memories are created, and that's usually the motivation. If it does turn out to be a good investment, that's a bonus.

Household Items

A 45-inch TV? A new bedroom suite? Snazzy cookware? A fully equipped workshop? These can't be considered investments because they don't increase in value, but they are the important rewards that will keep you motivated to stay on track for retirement. You can achieve them all, but probably not all at the same time.

Toys and Treats

Achievable on almost any budget are the little things that make life easier and more fun: cool software, great clothes, the latest skis—

what are yours? Put them on the wish list, then check your cash flow statement and see if there are some that you didn't know you cared so much about.

Activities

Almost everything costs money these days, so don't forget to list things like season tickets, Star Trek conferences, gym memberships and Sunday brunches.

New Car

A lot of my clients say they need a new car. Why? Public transit is inconvenient, and the old car is falling apart and costs too much to maintain. Or it might start falling apart soon. Or it's just a given that you should get a new car every three years. According to government studies, the average car costs $8,060 a year after tax (!) to maintain. If you have two cars in your family, you're eating up a big chunk of your disposable income. It's something to think about.

Things to Remember When Making Your Wish List

- Only you can make up your wish list. There are always tradeoffs and you'll only be willing to do the hard work of saving for the long term if there's a meaningful benefit in the short term.
- Find out what each item will cost, so that you will have specific dollar figures to aim for.
- If there are two of you, it's OK to have individual aims along with joint aims, as long as you come to an agreement on their priority.
- You can't Have It All Right Now, but if you're patient you can achieve everything over time.
- Recognize that if your list gets too long, you might not be able to achieve everything. I've found that the items that don't get fulfilled are the ones on the bottom of the list. Most people, once they see reality as revealed to them by the numbers, seem to accept it with grace: "I kinda knew it anyway."

YEARLY GOALS

Why bother with an annual list of personal goals? We only have 365 days a year and 24 hours a day. It seems like a lot when we're just embarking on the new year, but how often have you found yourself saying, "I can't believe it's November already!" Your goals keep you focused on what you want to achieve. They remind you that there are things that require your attention in the 365 fast-forward days to come. When that time is up—far sooner than you could have believed—you can look back and see that you've accomplished what you wanted to. That alone is invigorating and inspiring.

Some goals require financial planning. Want to work less? Quit working and stay home with the kids? Learn Spanish in Spain? Start your own business? You'll definitely need to lay the financial groundwork or your dream will remain out of reach.

Whether or not your goals have a direct bearing on your finances, they show you the big picture of what you want your life to be. That knowledge plays a big part in success. As my mom used to say, if you fail to plan, you plan to fail.

Many years ago I read an article about the work habits of Fortune 500 top executives, and all these alphas had three things in common:

1. Every evening, they made a list of the things they wanted to accomplish the next day.
2. They kept a notepad by the bed so that they could write down ideas that came to them at night.
3. Every year, they made a list of their goals for that year.

The article excited me. I did the first two things, the easy ones. I kept the pad by the bed and I made the list every night for the next day. I didn't bother with the last one, but it seemed like an OK idea, and I was in the business of giving advice, so I suggested to my clients that *they* make a yearly list of goals. After a while they started coming back telling me how excited they were about the whole process, and how making the list had clarified all sorts of issues for them. At this point—feeling pretty sheepish—I started to practise what I preached.

If you're not in the habit of writing down goals, I can only say that there's something magical about the process. It may seem like just a small step beyond "One of these days I really ought to . . ." but it's an important one. Somehow, in committing your goals and desires to paper, you're committing yourself to your goals and desires. For one thing, you've sat down and really thought about what you want to achieve. That gets your mind started, consciously or unconsciously, figuring out how to get it. It's amazing what your mind can get up to when you're not paying attention.

On top of that, you always have that reminder there to refocus you when you need it, and to show you what you've already accomplished.

People who like a lot of structure in their lives often resist this exercise because it seems a bit airy-fairy. They'd rather just get on with it. Creative people often resist because it seems too structured. That's because listing your yearly goals is structured creativity. It makes the structured types fantasize a bit and keeps the creative ones from leaving something unfinished when they flit off to the next thing. It also gives procrastinators and analyzers the nudge they need to just get on with it. I've had all kinds of people come back and tell me that once they got over their reluctance, it worked.

This isn't necessarily a financial exercise. Once you have your Enough number you'll be doing more detailed financial planning. Instead, right now you'll look at your life as a whole and see where you want to make improvements.

HOW TO SET YOUR YEARLY GOALS

I found that it took me a few years to get it right. At first I wrote down a few goals that were too difficult to accomplish in one year. I learned to take the really big goals and break them down into bite-sized pieces. I also learned what constitutes a goal and what doesn't. For instance, a friend and I like to make our lists together. One year I looked over at her list and thought, hey—that looks like a neat goal; I'll put that on my list! Then I added a few more of hers that looked interesting. Well, at the end of the year, to my surprise, the goals I had stolen from her ended up as orphans on my list. I realized that if I didn't own it, it simply wouldn't happen.

Over the years the lists themselves started inspiring new ideas. When I began, my goals were all involved with career and finances: how much money I wanted to earn, what courses I wanted to take to get to the next level, how to plan my day so I would have time to review. It took me a while to notice that only two areas of my life were represented on the list, so the next year I started to set some personal goals as well, like exercising more and becoming a better listener. After that I added relationship goals like calling up friends instead of waiting for them to call me. And as I added balance to my list, I gained balance in my life. In other words, setting goals actually changed my life.

I have found setting annual goals to be such an exciting exercise that I would never not do it. December is my time, but other people choose to do it on their birthdays. For some, September is a new start, or some need the quiet time of summer holidays when they have time to think. You can do the actual list-making alone or with an encouraging friend (not one who's going to pounce on you in six months and berate you for not finishing something you said you wanted to do). If you're half of a couple, don't feel that you have to share this activity with your mate. Your list is personal, almost like a diary. You only share it if you really want to. Keep it somewhere safe, maybe even somewhere special. You probably won't look at it often—although I know one woman who uses her list as a screen saver—but you'll want to know where to find it.

What Kinds of Goals Go on Your List?

Think in terms of four categories: personal, financial, career and relationships. These questions will get you started.

- What have I put off?
- What have I always wanted to try?
- What do I want to improve on?
- What do I want to experience?
- What do I want to share?
- What do I want to learn?
- What do I want to acquire?
- What do I want to give back?
- What do I want to let go of?

Be specific and keep your goals manageable. Instead of saying that you want to lose 30 pounds, aim to lose one pound a week until you've dropped 30. There are weeks when you won't achieve that, but most weeks you will, and you've got 52 weeks to reach your goal. Rather than saying you're going to develop new clients, say what kinds of clients you want to attract and what kind of work you want to do for them. Don't just write down that you're going to phone Mom more often; say how often, and when.

Some goals might go on your list for several years—not because they're unmanageable but because they're part of something ongoing. I want to become a better listener. I tend to start formulating my responses before the other person finishes talking, so instead of listening to her I'm listening to what's going on in my head. It's going to take me a while to get over that habit, forged as I was growing up in a household with nine brothers and sisters. So every year that little goal of self-improvement is there to remind me.

I find that as my December date draws near I'm busy formulating next year's goals in my head.When the time finally comes to write them down, I'm really excited about them and eager to get on with a new—and slightly different—year.

In the first three chapters, you've laid the groundwork for your Enough number. The Attitude Quiz, in Chapter 1 got the skeletons out of the closet. Understanding your attitude is understanding what can hold you back financially. In Chapter 2, your Cash Flow Statement gave you a cold, hard look at where your money really goes, and your Personal Balance Sheet showed you how close you are to your retirement goals. Your wish list and yearly goals from this chapter made you think about what you really want to achieve for yourself and acquire. So gather up all your lists and figures and let's find out how much is Enough, for you.

CHAPTER 4

WHAT'S ENOUGH FOR YOU— THE MAGIC NUMBER

I have enough money to last me the rest of my life . . . unless I buy something. — *Jackie Mason*

Sunshine sneaks through the cracks in the curtains. The sound of birds filters into your consciousness and gently wakes you. Mmmm. Is that the smell of coffee? Get a coffee, get ready for work . . . WORK! AAAAAAAGGGGHHH! Look at the TIME! I'm LATE! The ALARM didn't . . . oh . . . right.

You don't work anymore, remember? And you don't have to, because you have Enough. You knew how much you were aiming for, and you put away money faithfully, even though you occasionally had to deny yourself an immediate pleasure until you could afford it. Now, that money has multiplied so many times that it will provide for you for the rest of your life. So roll over and smile yourself back to sleep.

How much money do you need to enjoy that delicious moment one day? Lots of books and articles advise a flat $1 million. But if you want to maintain your penthouse in New York, the number may be more like $10 million. And if you're perfectly happy on $25,000 a year now, the figure might be $400,000.

What makes your Enough number different is that this is a completely customized calculation for you. It takes into account how much you must spend, how much you want to spend, how much you can save and what you want to do with it. Unlike standardized calculations, your Enough number gives you choices.

CRUNCHING THE NUMBERS

You've done the work, putting together your Cash Flow Statement (Figure 2.2) and your Personal Balance Sheet (Figure 2.4). Don't despair if computers or numbers aren't your thing. You now have all the tools you need to get someone else to calculate for you. You can take those figures to a bank or get a software program or see your financial planner to crunch the numbers and come up with your Enough number. It could cost you $500 to $1,000 to have this done by a financial advisor or an accountant. A bank will often do it for free or for a small fee. And if you go to **www.how-much-is-enough.com**, you can download the program I've developed—the one that's used for the calculations you'll see here.

Meet Thomas and Brenda

Thomas and Brenda will be our model couple as we go through the steps to find their Enough number. He's a 44-year-old self-employed electrician making $60,000 a year, with no pension plan. She's also 44-years-old, a schoolteacher making $30,000 on permanent part-time. Brenda has a small pension coming to her.

The house will be paid for when Thomas is 50, and the children will have graduated and left school. Janine is now in first year university and Justin is in grade 11. Aside from their RRSPs, they have RESPs for the children, but not a great deal of savings beyond those. They currently have $102,000 in RRSPs and contribute a total of $10,800 every year. In six years when the mortgage is paid off, they plan to put $500 of their $760 per month mortgage payment into non-RRSP investments, probably equity mutual funds. Thomas and Brenda are hoping to retire at 60. Their Total Expenditures Per Person After Retirement calculation (from Figure 2.3, page 29) tells them they'll need an after-tax income equivalent to $36,000 in today's dollars. Can you tell from Figure 4.1 whether or not they are on track?

PROJECTING FOR RETIREMENT

To find out if Thomas and Brenda are on track, we'll need to know how much they'll have to save by the time they're 60. A projection for retirement will estimate the *rate of inflation,* the *tax rate* and the *rate of return on investments.* I always make very conservative projections that leave lots of room for inflation but assume a fairly low rate of return on investments. For people 55 and under, I don't even include

Thomas and Brenda's
Figure 4.1:   Situation Summary

After-tax retirement income required: $36,000 (today's dollars)

Pre-tax retirement income required:

	THOMAS Current age: 44	BRENDA Current age: 44	TOTALS
Current RRSP balance	$82,000	$20,000	$102,000
Annual RRSP contribution	$10,800	$0	$10,800
Annual RRSP contribution room	$10,800	$0	$10,800
Current Non-RRSP balance	$0	$0	$0
Annual Non-RRSP contributions	$0	$0	$0
Future Non-RRSP contributions			$6,000 (from age 50)
Retirement pension		$5,700	$5,700

Canada Pension Plan and Old Age Security, because there's no way of knowing what shape those programs will be 10 years from now. It's a worst-case scenario, so if inflation is lower and/or the money earns more and/or CPP and OAS are still functioning, everything will look even better than the projection.

In finding your Enough number, you're taking your situation right now and making an informed guess. The closer you are to retirement, the more realistic this number will be. If you're younger, more changes will happen. But in all likelihood, the numbers will be even better when you retire, because you'll be doing a very conservative projection.

Some projections use pretty dubious numbers—a 10% or 12% rate of return on investments, for instance. I recommend that you use my very conservative estimates: 2% annual inflation rate and 6% annual return on your investments. If you've had consistent returns higher than 6%, you can adjust your projection, but I prefer to do a worst-case scenario.

> ## LOOK WHAT CAN HAPPEN OVER 30 YEARS
> George co-owned a grocery store. In the late 1950s, he remarked that the day he managed to earn $300 a month, he'd retire. Shortly after that, he and his partner took out partnership insurance in the amount of $300 a month, which would go to the survivor in case one of them died. Now *that* was security!
>
> Life went on. As inflation raged in the 1960s and '70s, it became obvious that nobody could retire on a few hundred bucks a month. The partner died. George kept working and saving, and his wife, Jean, invested their savings in blue chip stocks and reinvested the dividends. A few days after George's 65th birthday, he received a call from the company that had sold him the long-forgotten partnership insurance so many years ago, and a cheque for $300 started arriving monthly. It's a nice little bonus that makes up about one-sixth of George and Jean's monthly income of $2,000. Just imagine if the $300 were all that they had.

You can see from George and Jean's story how it pays to overestimate inflation and taxes and underestimate investment returns when you're projecting for your future. Your world is very different from theirs, of course—the value of your house might not increase by a factor of 10, as theirs has—but if you calculate from a worst-case scenario, you'll be on the safe side. (On the other hand, they could never have *dreamed* of paying $3.50 for a cup of coffee!)

With all that in mind, let's go through the steps to discover Thomas and Brenda's Enough number.

Step 1: Future Income Required

Figure 4.2 predicts how much income Thomas and Brenda will need per year to be comfortable in retirement.

Their Total Monthly Expenses After Retirement calculation from their Cash Flow Statement and When I Retire… (Figures 2.2 and 2.3, pages 27 and 29) tells them that they will need the equivalent of $3,000 a month, or $36,000 a year, after tax in today's money for a pleasant retirement. So we have to factor in inflation to find out the annual figures required for each year of retirement. Their tax bracket will be adjusted according to their income at retirement.

It's difficult enough to figure out this year's income tax, let alone estimate what it may be in the future. We don't know how much of Brenda and Thomas's retirement income will be taxed. We don't know if there will be any advantage to splitting income. The one thing that we can be sure of is that there will still be income tax. So, in light of all the unpredictable factors, we're assuming that all of their future income will be taxed at an average of 25%. This means that to have $36,000 right now they would have to have $48,000 coming in. Let's see what that means when Thomas and Brenda are 60.

Thomas and Brenda's
Figure 4.2: Future Income Requirements

FUTURE ANNUAL INCOME REQUIRED:
AFTER-TAX INCOME REQUIRED: 36,000

ASSUMPTIONS:
INFLATION RATE: 2.00%

AGE	ANNUAL REQUIREMENT	AGE	ANNUAL REQUIREMENT
44	36,000	57	46,570
45	36,720	58	47,501
46	37,454	59	48,451
47	38,203	**60**	**49,420**
48	38,968	61	50,409
49	39,747	62	51,417
50	40,542	63	52,445
51	41,353	64	53,494
52	42,180	**65**	**54,564**
53	43,023	66	55,655
54	43,884	67	56,768
55	44,761	68	57,904
56	45,657	69	59,062

Looking at Figure 4.2, you can see that Thomas and Brenda will need an annual income of $49,420 if they retire at 60, and that amount will increase by a little over $1,000 for each subsequent year of retirement. The next step is to determine how much money they will have by then.

Step 2: Principal at Retirement

Figure 4.3, Thomas and Brenda's Retirement Savings, demonstrates how much money they will have available when they retire at age 60. It starts by taking their current assets from their Personal Balance Sheet (Figure 2.4). This figure includes all their RRSP and non-RRSP investments. It doesn't include the value of their home, nor would it include the value of their vacation home (if they had one) unless they planned to sell it. If Thomas had a business that could be sold, the value of the business would be included, but as he *is* the business at the moment, there's nothing to sell.

Their current assets are broken down into RRSP and non-RRSP amounts. These will be compounded separately at a rate of 6%. The amount they save will be added every year and compounded at 6% as well. They will end up with an estimate of their principal at retirement age if they keep saving at the rate they plan.

Thomas and Brenda will have built a nest egg of $692,864 by the time they reach 60. If they start drawing $36,000 a year, how long will it last? Step 3 will tell us.

Step 3: Is it Enough?

This calculation uses the figures from Step 2 to predict how long Thomas and Brenda's savings will last. From retirement age on, the software program will calculate how much of their income will come from pensions and growth on their investments and how much will come from their principal. To be on the safe side, we're not including OAS or CPP here, because there is a small chance they won't be available by then. The program will subtract the principal as they pick away at it and tell us how old they will be when their principal runs out.

(I must add a note here. Many people are horrified at the thought of ever touching their principal. Okay Builders, Givers and Savers, I know you're going into resistance mode, but remember, all your life you've been told to save, and this is what you were saving for. This exercise is especially important for you so you'll see that, using these conservative estimates, you will never run out of money. At retirement, you have arrived. You may have to draw on your principal, but that's the whole idea. If you're concerned about leaving a nest egg behind, you can make that happen, and you'll learn how in Chapter 12 when I'll explain estate planning.)

Figure 4.3:   Thomas and Brenda's Retirement Savings (retirement at age 60)

CURRENT AGE: 44

INVESTMENT INFORMATION:
CURRENT NON-RRSP AMOUNT: 0
CURRENT RRSP AMOUNT: 102,000

ASSUMPTIONS:
INTEREST RATE: 6.00%
INFLATION RATE: 2.00%

Age	RRSP Balance	Annual RRSP Savings	RRSP Growth	Year-End RRSP Balance	Annual Non-RRSP Savings	After Tax Growth	Year-End Non-RRSP Balance	Total Year-End
44	102,000	10,800	6,768	119,568	0	0	0	119,568
45	119,568	10,800	7,822	138,190	0	0	0	138,190
46	138,190	10,800	8,939	157,929	0	0	0	157,929
47	157,929	10,800	10,124	178,853	0	0	0	178,853
48	178,853	10,800	11,379	201,032	0	0	0	201,032
49	201,032	10,800	12,710	224,542	0	0	0	224,542
50	224,542	10,800	14,121	249,463	6,000	360	6,360	255,823
51	249,463	10,800	15,616	275,879	6,000	742	13,102	288,980
52	275,879	10,800	17,201	303,879	6,000	1,146	20,248	324,127
53	303,879	10,800	18,881	333,560	6,000	1,575	27,823	361,383
54	333,560	10,800	20,662	365,022	6,000	2,029	35,852	400,874
55	365,022	10,800	22,549	398,371	6,000	2,511	44,363	442,734
56	398,371	10,800	24,550	433,721	6,000	3,022	53,385	487,106
57	433,721	10,800	26,671	471,193	6,000	3,563	62,948	534,141
58	471,193	10,800	28,920	510,912	6,000	4,137	73,085	583,997
59	510,912	10,800	31,303	553,015	6,000	4,745	83,830	636,845
60	**553,015**	**10,800**	**33,829**	**597,644**	**6,000**	**5,390**	**95,220**	**692,864**

How Long will Thomas and Brenda's Retirement Savings Last?

Figure 4.4:   (retirement at age 60)

RETIREMENT AGE: 60

INVESTMENT CAPITAL: 692,864

| PENSION INCOME: | Monthly: $475 | Yearly: $5,700 |
| INCOME REQUIRED: | Monthly: $4,547 | Yearly: $49,420 |

ASSUMPTIONS:
INTEREST RATE: 6.00%
MARGINAL TAX RATE: 25.00%
INFLATION RATE: 2.00%

Age	Capital	Income From Investment	After Tax Income	After Tax Pension Income Indexed	Total Income	After Tax Income Required	(Deficit/ Surplus From Capital)
60	692,864	41,572	31,179	4,275	35,454	49,420	-13,966
61	678,898	40,734	30,550	4,361	34,911	50,408	-15,497
62	663,400	39,804	29,853	4,448	34,301	51,417	-17,116
63	646,285	38,777	29,083	4,537	33,619	52,445	-18,825
64	627,459	37,648	28,236	4,627	32,863	53,494	-20,631
65	606,828	36,410	27,307	4,720	32,027	54,564	-22,536
66	584,292	35,058	26,293	4,814	31,107	55,655	-24,547
67	559,744	33,585	25,189	4,911	30,099	56,768	-26,669
68	533,076	31,985	23,988	5,009	28,997	57,903	-28,906
69	504,169	30,250	22,688	5,109	27,797	59,061	-31,265
70	472,905	28,374	21,281	5,211	26,492	60,243	-33,751

Age	Capital	Income From Investment	After Tax Income	After Tax Pension Income Indexed	Total Income	After Tax Income Required	(Deficit)/ Surplus From Capital
71	439,154	26,349	19,762	5,315	25,077	61,448	-36,370
72	402,784	24,167	18,125	5,422	23,547	62,677	-39,130
73	363,654	21,819	16,364	5,530	21,895	63,930	-42,035
74	321,619	19,297	14,473	5,641	20,114	65,209	-45,095
75	276,524	16,591	12,444	5,754	18,197	66,513	-48,316
76	228,208	13,692	10,269	5,869	16,138	67,843	-51,705
77	176,503	10,590	7,943	5,986	13,929	69,200	-55,271
78	121,232	7,274	5,455	6,106	11,561	70,584	-59,023
79	62,209	3,733	2,799	6,228	9,027	71,996	-62,968
80	-760	0	0	6,352	6,352	73,436	-67,083

Figure 4.5: Thomas and Brenda's Retirement Savings (retirement at age 65)

Age	RRSP Balance	Annual RRSP Savings	RRSP Growth	Year-End RRSP Balance	Annual Non-RRSP Savings	After Tax Growth	Year-End Non-RRSP Balance	Total Year-End
60	**553,015**	**10,800**	**33,829**	**597,644**	**6,000**	**5,390**	**95,220**	**692,864**
61	597,644	10,800	36,507	644,951	6,000	6,073	107,293	752,243
62	644,951	10,800	39,345	695,096	6,000	6,798	120,090	815,186
63	695,096	10,800	42,354	748,249	6,000	7,565	133,656	881,905
64	748,249	10,800	45,543	804,592	6,000	8,379	148,035	952,627
65	804,592	10,800	48,924	864,316	6,000	9,242	163,277	1,027,593

Step 4: Then What *is* Enough?

If Thomas and Brenda retire at 60, they will run out of their own money when they're 79, leaving them with only her small pension. If OAS and CPP are still around, their money will last a few years longer and they'll also have that extra income when their own funds run out. Either way, it looks as though they'll have to make some changes.

By the time the mortgage is paid off they won't be supporting two kids anymore, so maybe at that stage they could start living on their projected retirement income, or just a little more, and really sock it away for a few years to assure themselves a *very* comfortable retirement. Or they could work for an extra five years and they could keep saving at the rate they've set for themselves. We have the technology to find out exactly what they'll need to do to achieve the retirement they dream about. Let's go back and see what happens to them if Brenda and Thomas work an extra five years to age 65. We'll start by going back to Step 2 and recalculating their Principal at Retirement, as shown in Figure 4.5.

With an extra five years of work, without even increasing their savings, Thomas and Brenda have upped their retirement principal by over $300,000! Is that going to take them over the top? We'll run through Step 3 again and find out. Figure 4.6 shows how long Thomas and Brenda's retirement savings will last if they work an extra five years to age 65. To make the chart a little shorter, the calculations are given in five-year increments.

Ah, now that's more like it. With these conservative projections, Brenda and Thomas should be okay until they're 94. And at that point, they still have the capital left from their home. If they're not comfortable with that, they can run their numbers again and see what would happen if they invested an extra $100 or $200 a month after they've finished paying off their mortgage. Or maybe Thomas still wants to retire at 60. How much more will they have to put away to make that possible? By playing with their Enough number, they will know exactly what they have to do now to have the life they want when they retire. And so can you. Your Enough number gives you the guidelines and you decide on the tradeoffs.

WHAT YOUR ENOUGH NUMBER MEANS

Once you've determined your Enough number, you can see exactly where you stand now. Then you can apply different scenarios and see how a bit

How Long will Thomas and Brenda's Retirement Savings Last?

Figure 4.6: (retirement at age 65)

RETIREMENT AGE: 65

INVESTMENT CAPITAL: $1,027,593

PENSION INCOME:	Monthly: $475	Yearly: $5,700
INCOME REQUIRED:	Monthly: $4,547	Yearly: $54,564

ASSUMPTIONS:
INTEREST RATE: 6.00%
MARGINAL TAX RATE: 25.00%
INFLATION RATE: 2.00%

Age	Capital	Income From Investment	After Tax Income	After Tax Pension Income Indexed	Total Income	After Tax Income Required	(Deficit)/ Surplus From Capital
65	1,027,593	61,656	46,242	4,275	50,517	54,564	-4,047
70	994,723	59,683	44,763	4,720	49,482	60,243	-10,761
75	923,594	55,416	41,562	5,109	46,671	66,513	-19,842
80	801,942	48,117	36,087	5,641	41,728	73,436	-31,708
85	614,015	36,841	27,631	6,228	33,859	81,079	-47,221
90	339,716	20,383	15,287	6,876	22,163	89,518	-67,355
95	-46,392	0	0	7,592	7,592	98,835	-91,243

of tweaking will change your situation. For instance, if you increased your savings by $50 a month, how much earlier could you retire? If your savings will only last until you're 70, how much more do you need to save per year to take care of yourself to age 90? If you decide to live on less income when you retire, how long will it take you to get to where you need to be? What's the difference between keeping your summer cabin and selling it? Or, if you're young and expect to be making more money in a few years, how much will you have to save to continue at your projected monthly income? Just download the program from **www.how-much-is-enough.com** or take your figures from Chapter 2 to a financial planner, accountant, bank or credit union.

IF YOU'RE ON TRACK

If your current level of saving will get you there, fabulous. Stop reading now and give this book to a friend. You're fine. (Or you could just peek at the chapters on investing to see how to build your savings even more.) Relax and start thinking about your wish list.

Nothing makes me happier than to meet people who are doing everything right and can start to enjoy that little bit extra. In fact, I developed this program for people who had enough money and didn't know it—an older generation who had been squirrelling away money all their lives and were afraid to spend any of it. They had grown up in the Depression and knew what it was like not to have enough. This program was a way to show them that, yes, they did have enough, and now they should start enjoying it.

It all fell into place one day when I received a very sad phone call from a client. She and her husband, a doctor, had come to see me because he had retired and they worried that they might not have enough to live on. I looked at their situation and had the rare pleasure of telling them that not only were they fine, but they couldn't even spend all the interest, much less go through the principal.

When I told them that it was time to start indulging themselves, the idea really went against the grain. They were both Savers by nature, and the Depression had made them ultra-cautious. Finally I ran their Enough number to show them. When at last they believed me, I persuaded them to book a first-class flight to Italy to go and visit their son, who worked there. They left the office and booked the trip that day. A few days later, the doctor suffered a catastrophic heart attack and died. All that saving, and no chance to share the pleasures they could have so easily afforded.

One of my favourite people has been diagnosed with Alzheimer's disease, but he can take comfort in the fact that he and his wife did everything they wanted to before it happened—all because they knew that they had Enough.

If you are on track, you have the tools now to help you make your Wish List become a reality even quicker, and I urge you to do so. You *can* indulge yourself without sacrificing your peace of mind. Congratulations.

IF YOU'RE NOT ON TRACK

I had a couple who were nearing retirement but couldn't *possibly* save any money, even though they had virtually nothing put away. There was no limit to the things they could find to spend their money on. Nothing I did or said seemed to help them understand the crisis they were in. Finally I found the right button to push. I asked them "If you can't live on $90,000 a year now, how do you expect to live on $20,000 after you're retired?"

Ask yourself the same question.

If you need to save more to get to your Enough number, you have to stop spending more than you make. You can't even spend everything you make. Eventually you won't make any more. You have to plan for that day. So you have two choices: spend less, or make more. What's it going to be? It's scary, I know. But at least you're better off than you were before you started reading this book.

You know more about yourself. Your attitude toward money isn't going to change, and now that you've discovered what it is, you can avoid the pitfalls common to your type. You've also examined your goals and wishes, so you know what you really want.

You know where your money goes. You've tracked every cent, and you've seen where your spending habits get in the way of your desires. You've determined your bottom-line needs and can start making priorities for whatever's left.

You know how much is Enough. Now that you have your Enough number you know where you stand, for better or worse. Isn't it a relief to have a specific amount of money to aim for? Even if you're behind in your savings or struggling with debt, at least you know exactly what it will take to fix your situation. You can do it.

In Part Two I'll show you how to get out of debt, save money, invest wisely and pay less in taxes. Start now and you'll be astonished at how quickly you can achieve financial freedom. Pretty soon, you'll be enjoying some of the items on your wish list.

Part 2

GETTING ENOUGH

There are no rules for getting rich quick. There are, however, rules for getting rich slowly.

CHAPTER

GETTING ON TRACK

I think I can, I think I can, I think I can. — The Little Engine That Could

At this moment, you're closer to getting Enough than you ever have been. It was a bit of a struggle, but now you know exactly what Enough is, and exactly how much money you need to put away to get there. If you're in debt or you need to save more to get to it, don't be discouraged. You're on your way. There's no going back now because you have the knowledge. Even if it's not a smooth road ahead, at least you know where you're going.

If you're not on track, you're ready for some tough love. When you buy something, do you need it, or merely want it? Are you spending all your disposable income on wants and not covering your needs? Before you start giving yourself treats and rewards, you need to take the right amount off the top of your earnings first, to reach your Enough number and cover your necessities. Now it's up to you to determine what you have to give up to get that money.

So many people come to me with the have-to-haves: "our daughter has to have her school trip"; "we have to have another car"; "I can't function without taking classes . . ." Unfortunately, if you don't have the money, you've got to get it from someone else—a bank, a relative, a credit card company, a (former) friend. And then you end up paying other people interest, which, essentially is money that you could be enjoying. That interest paid to someone else could be a vacation for you and your family, piano lessons for your kids or money you couldn't find for your retirement. Why let someone else profit from your confusion?

NEEDS VS. WANTS

Difficult as it is to adjust to the fact, if you can't afford it, you don't *have to have* it. There are only a few things you really have to have, and they are listed here. So take a deep breath and list your needs and how much they cost per month. Once you can cover your needs, you can play with the rest, but not before. Your real needs are:

- **Shelter.** Either rent or mortgage, property taxes, heat, electricity and water. This does not include gardeners, household help, swimming pools or vacation homes. Those will improve your quality of life if you can afford them. If you can't, they'll stress you out.
- **Home repairs, renovation.** Your home is your biggest investment. It increases the resale value to keep it in good repair and up-to-date. But not all improvements are necessary. Before embarking on any renovation, ask first if you'll be able to get most of that money back when you sell. Then ask if you can afford it right now without too much hardship. If you can't, don't. Renovations are stressful enough without money worries too. It's not worth the grief.
- **Food.** Within reason. Much as you may like to dine on fresh white truffles from Italy, you could survive without them. Dinner parties and restaurant meals count as entertainment, not food (unless you can write them off—but that still costs you 75¢ on the dollar).
- **Clothing.** You know the level of dress you need to suit your position. I had a client who had been spending $1,000 a month on clothes in her campaign to attract a husband. I diverted most of that money to a down payment on a condo, and she still had so many clothes she didn't need to repeat an outfit for over a month. She got the husband too. (He was attracted by her real estate.)
- **Children's current needs.** This one's tough, because who can make a better case of desperate need than a style-deprived teenager? You're the grownup, so you get to decide what's a need and what's a want, but as a rule of thumb, current school supplies, a reasonable wardrobe that fits, and enough food count as needs. Private schooling, lessons, camps and sports expenses are wants— high priority ones, but wants just the same. And when it comes to a new snowboard or the entire Pokémon collection—no question.

- **Children's future education.** We want our children to have more opportunities than we had. Selfishly speaking, there's a lot of peace of mind that comes from seeing our little responsibilities launched and taking care of themselves. Not everyone will be able to pay the children's full post-secondary education—not everyone wants to—but parents will be called upon to provide resources, financial and otherwise, for their children's education. There can certainly be hard decisions here. RESPs save you tax as you save for their university, college or vocational school. Read more about them in Chapter 8.

- **Retirement.** Unless you have some good reason to believe that you won't be around by then, you'd better save at least something for retirement: 10% of your gross annual income right off the top. Meanwhile the tax break from Registered Retirement Saving Programs (RRSPs) and contributions to pension plans give you more disposable income to pay down debt, contribute to the children's education or achieve other dreams.

- **Insurance.** If other people depend on you, don't take a chance on leaving them high and dry if you *don't* make it to retirement. If you're the chief breadwinner and/or self-employed, make certain your family can continue on without hardship. And if you're self-employed, you can't be without disability insurance. More on insurance in Chapters 9 and 10.

- **Taxes.** I know, I know. They're one of the more infuriating facts of life, but I can't imagine anything less pleasurable than paying taxes *and* paying interest on them. Pay the darn things up front and try to forget the misery.

- **Pay down debt.** Interest payments bring no pleasure and no satisfaction. You're just handing over your money to someone else. Less debt means fewer interest payments, which means more money left in your pocket to get what you want. And if you ever find yourself in a financial bind, from illness, a pay cut or loss of your job, less debt is always easier to manage. The sooner you pay down debt, the sooner you get to keep all your after-tax money and start to enjoy it, and the sooner you'll be doing all that work for yourself and your family. The banks will just have to get along without you.

Not very exciting, are they? But knowing how much your needs cost every month will give you an idea of the bare minimum you'll need when you retire—and how much disposable income you have now. Time to budget the flexible items, your wants.

BUDGETING—I'LL TRY TO BE GENTLE

Budget. The word makes a lot of people run screaming. There are Spenders, Builders and Givers with bad cases of the have-to-haves. They can't possibly budget. If they can't have everything they want, exactly when they want it, well life just isn't worth living. That's all fine if they can really afford it. If they can't, the whirling blades will chew them up.

There's another side to budgeting, too. For many people, the most they're able to do is to put food on the table and pay the mortgage. Anything else seems out of the question. When their kids plead for the latest cool shoes, it cuts the parents deeply to say no. They don't want to set their kids apart—other kids can be brutal. So if Mom and Dad can't even handle that little extra bit, where are they going to get the money to save for retirement?

Believe me, there are ways. I have seen people do amazing things when they set their priorities.

Very early in my career I met a couple with three kids. They managed on his salary, which would now be about $33,000. With that, they managed to buy a townhouse in a nice neighbourhood and even save money. It was important for her to stay home with the kids, so she planted a vegetable garden and cooked all of their meals. She made many of the kids' clothes and bought the rest of the family clothing at upscale second-hand shops where the clothing was very good and seldom worn. The kids had to pay for their own college tuition and supplies by getting summer jobs and scholarships, but they were able to live at home the whole time for free.

It impressed me—surprised me even—that these people could do so much on so little; however they knew what they wanted and they stayed focused. Their goal was to be a family.

I've also seen some great turnarounds. One couple lived on $80,000 and spent almost every cent they earned. They had a house and a few savings. They weren't living a life of luxury, just being eaten up by little expenses: buying a lot of gifts, going to the theatre, eating out. It was also important to them to pay for as much of their kids' university

education as they could handle. They weren't saving for their retirement, even though it wasn't that far away. When we ran their numbers,
it became clear where their money was going.

I also did some projections for them based on different levels of saving. They got excited about the compounding effect when they saw it on
paper. They started from the top down and figured out how much they
wanted to save, then just did it. He started taking the bus to work and eating a bag lunch. They stopped buying books and magazines and started
going to the library. They stopped giving extravagant gifts. When I asked
them if any of the cutbacks had been a hardship, they said no; if anything,
some things had ended up being better.

The first thing they did was pay down their mortgage as quickly as
possible. That gave them money to put in their RRSPs, so they used the
carry-forward to max them out as quickly as they could. Then they were
able to save outside their RRSPs as well, and even enjoy the odd treat, like
a vacation. Their positive attitude and motivation made it all possible.

These two will be okay in retirement. In fact, they've even started living at the same level as their projected retirement income so they'll have
more of a cushion. The other day I told them how proud I was of them and
they just beamed. It took them all of eight years to get on track for retirement. It's never too late.

THE TEN PERCENT RULE

Want to get out of debt, retire comfortably and make your dreams come
true? Two words: *ten percent*. Take 10% off the top of your gross earnings, no matter how much or how little you earn. Take it off before you
can spend it, and pay down your debt or put it in a GIC or mutual fund. If
your employer has a savings plan, be part of it. Put the money in your
RRSPs, and a percentage will be returned to you in tax savings, which you
can then invest.

Put that first 10% away the minute you get the cheque, or, better yet,
have it taken off *before* you get the cheque. You won't even know it's
gone, and you won't believe how quickly it will build up. At the end of a
year, you will have saved over a month's earnings.

The first time is the most difficult, especially if you're young and not
making much money, but after a while you won't even notice. Just try to
keep in mind how fast your savings are accumulating. And when that

$100 raise comes, take 10% off the top and you've still got 90 more dollars than you had before.

Later on, when you're living comfortably within your means, boost your automatic savings to 15% or 20% to assure a retirement in which you can do whatever you want.

FINDING THE MONEY TO SAVE

Don't stop reading just because you're in debt. It's not a terminal condition. Now is the time to take a hard look at your Cash Flow Statement (Figure 2.2) and see what expenses can be cut down or eliminated.

So far I've only hinted at cutting down expenses, for fear of scaring you. But now that you've scared yourself, I can open up a bit. As I've mentioned, if you need to find ways to save money, you either need to spend less or make more. Which is easier?

I thought so. Yes, you might hit it big in soybean futures—but that's gambling, not earning. (Check out Chapter 7 for some wisdom on various kinds of investing.) Yes, you might find a new job that doubles your pay. And, yes, you might even win the lottery. But not spending money can make a difference immediately.

Clear Up Debt

Paying down debt *is* saving. Look back through your credit card bills or linc-of-credit statements and add up all the interest you've spent. What could you have bought with that money? Get rid of that interest. Keep your money for yourself. Build a cushion in case of emergency. Start saving for the things you really want.

I know this is hard, especially when you get letters every week telling you that you're pre-approved for the latest low-interest, extra-bonus-points precious-metal credit cards, or a higher limit on your line of credit. Hey, you're pre-approved; you must be able to afford it, right? Especially if you're maxed out. Spenders, Builders and Givers can be mightily tempted by credit. If you're one of them, please resist. The credit card companies wouldn't be after you if they didn't think they were going to make money off you.

Even Savers can have a problem if they get into debt. I've had clients who owe thousands of dollars, and also have some money put away. When I tell them to put the savings toward the debt, they're horrified. If they do that they won't have any savings at all! It does seem counterintuitive to spend savings you already have in order to save more, but it works. In all but the rarest of circumstances, your savings are not earning as much in interest as you're paying on your debts. When you use the savings to pay down the debt, you decrease your monthly installment, which leaves you more money to pay down the rest of the debt. Once you've paid it off, you can start saving again—only this time you get to keep it all.

MAKING THE MOST OF THEIR MONEY

Caroline and Yoshi were paying $1,000 a month on a car loan and an RRSP loan. But they also had money saved for a future trip to visit his family in Japan, and some bonds that they thought of as an emergency fund. It took a lot of persuading, but finally they used their savings to pay off their two loans. Two things happened. Now they could save the $1,000 they had been paying out and it was all theirs. And they were able to max out the next year's RRSPs without taking out a loan. Within 14 months they had all the savings they had started out with, and no debt. They were using their money more efficiently.

Pay off your highest-interest debts first, then move to the next highest. Make a list of all your outstanding balances and the interest rate you're paying on each. Take the figures to your bank and ask if it makes sense to get a loan to consolidate all your debt. But there's a rule. You only get to do this once. When you've paid off your debt, you can't start building it up again. You need to start to spend less than you earn instead of more.

If your Cash Flow Statement tells you you're spending too much for what you're making, getting rid of your debt is your first and most important step. Don't wait for that Oh-No moment when you realize you're in too deep.

Control Impulse Buying

Are you a Spender—one of the crow people attracted by bright, shiny objects? Or a Giver with no defence against a sad story? A Builder who spots new opportunities everywhere? There's a wonderful world of temptation out there. First there were stores, then malls, then direct mail, then catalogues, then the Home Shopping Channel, now the Internet—all vying for your attention and your dollars. What to do?

If your earning power doesn't equal your yearning power, you need to play some tricks on your inner wild child. Here are some suggestions:

- **Restrict yourself to one credit card.** One monthly bill showing everything you've charged—now *that's* a reality check. Choose the card with the lowest interest rate and cut up the rest. You don't need more than one for your personal purchases. If you're self-employed, carry another one exclusively for business purchases.
- **Double the price.** When you buy something, you're paying for it with after-tax dollars and you're paying sales tax on top of the price. If you made $42,000 last year, you hit the 40% tax bracket. Now you're going to have to spend up to 8% in provincial sales tax and another 7% for GST. So in order to buy something, you have to earn at least twice the sticker price. Think of all those extra hours you spent gazing into that computer screen, or digging that dirt, or driving that truck, and ask yourself if you really want it that badly.
- **Wait awhile.** When you see something you want, wait 48 hours before you buy it. My clients who do this tell me that 90% of the time they've forgotten about it two days later. Sellers make products more desirable by indicating that they won't be available at this price forever, or that the quantities are limited. It's an old trick, but it gets hands reaching for wallets every time. Keep in mind that a bargain is only a bargain when you save money on something you planned to buy in the first place.
- **Agree on it.** When it comes to couples, sometimes one person is the impulse buyer; sometimes both are. Once the two of you have agreed that you need to save more money, make a deal: before either of you spends over a certain amount, say $100 or $200, you both have to agree on the purchase. This way you can avoid those unfortunate "Hey honey, come out and listen to the cool new sound system I got for the car" discussions—or at least you can have them before the money is spent.
- **Don't leave home with it.** Leave your credit card, chequebook and debit card at home when you go out. Carry enough cash for what you need and spend that. Remember cash? I know people who rationalize using their credit card for everything because they receive airline points, but until you can manage to use your credit card for only the things you need or plan, and you're able to pay it off in full at the end of every month, forget the points. It's too easy to use them as an excuse for spending. In fact, just carrying a

credit card encourages you to spend money because you think you
have it when you don't. Using cash reminds you that you're dealing with actual money.

- **Set a limit.** You know how much your needs cost each month. The
  flip side is that you also know what's left over for stuff you want.
  Put your fun money in a separate bank account, and use only that
  account for your wants. Again, if you spend it only in cash you'll
  be able to keep a running account, both in your wallet and on
  your bank statements. If it's the 21st and you've only got 16 discretionary dollars to take you to the end of the month, you'll suddenly hit new levels of creative frugality.
- **Keep a record.** If you're really having trouble staying within
  your budget, try to continue keeping a record the way you did
  when you were working on your Cash Flow Statement. When you
  have to stop and write down every purchase as you make it, you
  might think about your spending a little more. And as you watch
  your purchases adding up, you can spot when you're getting too
  close to the edge.

Cut Costs

Okay, but where??? If you're living at the limit and you don't think you're
spending to excess, is there anywhere you can cut costs? Well, you may
have to give up something you're used to. And it will seem difficult. The
upside is that as you spend less, you're saving more. You may learn to get
some fun out of that fact alone.

Let's look in the obvious places first.

VACATIONS

Somewhere along the line we decided that if we weren't lounging on
some tropical island or climbing an unknown peak or cruising on an ocean
liner, we weren't having fun. Travel is no good unless it's far away. The
kids will wither and die if they don't get to Disneyland. Even camping is
no good unless it involves a satellite TV and a microwave.

Think back. Did your parents do all that, or was your big family vacation a driving trip to see the relatives? It *is* possible to have fun without
spending a bundle. Maybe Mexico instead of Maui, or a condo instead of
a hotel room so you don't have to eat every meal in a restaurant. Can you
substitute a flight to a faraway place with a driving vacation close to home?
How about restricting yourself to one trip a year instead of two or three?

One of my favourite holidays was two weeks at home. I told everyone I was gone, then hiked, wandered, hung out, dined, explored and enjoyed my own city through the eyes of a tourist. It was fun, it was zero stress and it was far less money than I would have spent going somewhere. No jet lag, either. Many of my clients who have been working their way out of debt have tried the same thing, and they've always been delighted—not only about the money they saved, but with the experience itself.

Exotic vacations are wonderful, but you can have a great time in less expensive places too. If vacations are putting you over the top, cutting back on the number or the expense is a fairly painless way of saving.

ACTIVITIES

Season tickets, club memberships, recreation, entertainment and hobbies can become burdens when they compete with needs. Because these give so much pleasure, no one gives them up willingly. However, you may have to modify your spending on them while you get caught up.

With both season tickets and club memberships, ask yourself if you're really using and enjoying them and if they're worth giving up something else for. If you simply can't give them up entirely, can you cut back somehow?

Season tickets to anything are getting so expensive that many loyal fans or concert-goers who have been subscribing for years find they can no longer afford a whole season. Unfortunately, that often means giving up their favourite seats and the companionship of the people seated around them. One solution that works well is to split the cost among several people and go in turns.

Club memberships are another tough one. In some clubs, if you drop out, you may not get back in again. Golf and other recreational clubs often offer less expensive social memberships that allow you to use the social facilities but "pay to play."

Recreation, entertainment and hobby costs can sneak up because they're spread throughout the year. Your Cash Flow Statement (Figure 2.2) shows you how much you're spending on these. How much of that do you want to save? Allot yourself a budget and stick to it. It may mean cross-country skiing instead of downhill, or potluck dinners in place of restaurant entertaining, but you won't stop enjoying yourself; you'll just be doing it in a different way. There's also a certain amount of satisfaction in knowing that the money you're not spending now will help you in the future.

LITTLE THINGS THAT ADD UP

"Did I really spend $200 a month on lattès?" "It was just a few little gifts; I couldn't have spent *that* much." "Why am I paying $600 a year for magazines I don't have time to read?" "If I spent this much on clothes, how come I *still* don't have anything to wear?"

You found a few surprises in your Cash Flow Statement, didn't you? Now's the time to decide whether you give up these expenses and save the money, or treat yourself and give up something else. The criterion is enjoyment. Are the lattès just an expensive way of getting your coffee buzz, or do you savour the atmosphere of the coffee bar and think great thoughts as the chocolate sprinkles sink into the foam? Are you willing to give up something else for your daily beanfest? You might have already been through this exercise on your Wish List, but now we're at the crunch.

If you decide to cut back on your treats, here are a few words and phrases that might help: library, Thermos, from scratch, secondhand, off-season, homemade, borrow, rent, brown bag, fix, 50% off, do it yourself, not right now, do without. Don't know if I've covered absolutely everything in this short list, but it's a good start. (If your immediate reaction to that list is "I'd rather die a pauper!" all I can say is, if you don't do some of this stuff, you just might.)

LUXURY LIVING

It's possible to bring in six figures a year and still go broke. Mansions, private schools, household help and high style are status symbols precisely because most people can't afford them. Yet for those who want to project an image of carefree wealth, they're have-to-haves.

The most amazing coincidence happened a few years ago in my office. Robert, who lived in a wealthy neighbourhood, came to me with some big worries. He had his mortgage paid off and was well on track for retirement, but he thought he must be doing something wrong. Maybe he needed to be investing more aggressively or something, because the guy across the street, who was in the same business and probably at about the same income level, seemed to have so much more. That guy had twin Range Rovers, a ski cabin, expensive renovations, luxury vacations—the whole deal.

I hear worries like that all the time. I tried to reassure Robert. He was doing fine, after all, and his investments were working nicely. I said that he had to make decisions based on his own needs and wants, not on comparisons with other people.

That same week, the guy across the street came into my office. He was on the verge of bankruptcy and didn't know what to do.

If it's important to you to project an image of wealth, remember to balance your have-to-haves with what you can afford. Remember too, that no one but you demands that you spend conspicuously.

IF YOU'VE CUT ALL YOU CAN AND IT'S STILL NOT ENOUGH

The cost-cutting measures I've already talked about are the easy ones— cutting out or cutting down the luxuries, big and small. Maybe that's not enough. Or maybe you were never able to indulge in those things in the first place. Now our flinty-eyed look at your finances becomes a squint. You may have to make some serious changes.

Transportation

It costs around $8,060 a year to run a car, on average.[1] If you have two, is there any way you can get along with one? If you have one and hardly ever use it, can you get rid of it? If you're making payments on a luxury late-model vehicle, would you consider selling it and buying a cheaper car that you can own outright?

We North Americans just lo-o-o-ove our cars, and as often as not, these questions are greeted with a shocked gasp, as if I had suggested selling the children. After all, car or not, transportation still costs money, and for most of us, the $8,060 is worth it in sheer convenience. But if you're struggling, this might be where you can save a few thousand dollars. You'll get money from the sale, which you can use immediately to pay down debt; and you'll wipe out the continuing costs of gas, parking, insurance and maintenance. Eight thousand and sixty dollars would pay for a lot of bus, carpool and taxi rides, and a few weekend car rentals too—with money to spare.

If you customarily buy a new car every three years, you'll save money by keeping your car longer. With good maintenance, a car should last 10 years or more before running into major repairs, and that gives you time to save up for your next one. It can even be a luxury car, once you have your finances in order.

---

1 Based on a mid-size, four-cylinder American car driven for 18,000 kilometres per year.

Home

Even if it's still mortgaged, this is your biggest asset, and the one you can least afford to do without. My first suggestion is always to make it work for you. Could you take in a student boarder or two to help with the mortgage, or put a suite in the basement to rent out? You'll have to do some research before you try this, finding out about insurance, landlord/tenant rules, safety and costs for improvements.

Only as a last resort do I suggest selling your house and buying a cheaper one, but sometimes it is necessary. One couple I worked with had built up a horrendous debt, and a big part of it was their $400,000 mortgage. They could barely function at work because they were becoming immobilized from all the stress. Even their children were feeling it. Yet the couple couldn't see their way out. They had an image to uphold, only they couldn't afford the image they were upholding. Regretfully, they put their house on the market, and when it sold they bought another. Their mortgage was now a much more manageable $150,000. Instant stress relief.

A final word: be very careful of home equity loans. Home equity loans are worthwhile for necessary repairs. They can also be useful if a) you're making improvements that will increase the value of your home and you expect to get the money back when you sell, and b) you're not in debt when you take out the loan. Improvements that won't add to the resale value are wish list items, and you are far better off if you save for them. (If your mortgage leaves you no room to save, you should be thinking about a less expensive home, not doing elective surgery on the one you have.) And don't even think about taking out a home equity loan to buy a car, or any other item that depreciates.

It's tempting to add a few more years to your mortgage to get what you want now, but ask to see what the interest will cost. Remember, that's all money that you won't get to spend on goodies.

If you're a Giver, Spender or Builder who's lost a bit of control, making these changes can feel like a terrible burden, I know. You're used to using your credit to get what you want now, and worrying about it later. The trouble is, you've taken on a whole lot of worry. At some point, it's going to haunt you. If you're ready to shake off that worry, make compound interest work for you instead of against you and you'll start to see a difference immediately. Once you start to keep your own money, you can make it grow. And you know what? You don't have to do it alone. In the next chapter I'll explore the advantages of having a financial planner—someone who can cheer you on and guide you through the increasingly complex array of investment choices and tax complications.

CHAPTER

FINDING FINANCIAL ADVICE

Teachers open the door, but you must enter by yourself.
— *Chinese proverb*

As a non-professional, you can probably save and invest wisely, but you might be missing chances to save tax or fees, or to take advantage of new opportunities. The more information out there, the more confusing it all gets. The tax system, the legal system and the multitude of new investment choices can make your head reel, so please consider getting help. You don't have to be rich to have a financial planner. This stuff is complicated.

Over the course of my years in the business, I have seen an incredible bloom of new investment vehicles, saving schemes and forms of taxation. It's a full-time job keeping up with them all. It also takes experience to incorporate all that information into each client's individual investment plan. People thought that all the information available on the Internet would make investing a cakewalk, but a friend of mine, after ploughing through a lot of it suggested that each Internet screen should come with a little note at the bottom: Wisdom Sold Separately.

A good financial advisor provides the wisdom. Quite often, clients come to me with a snippet about investing they've read in a magazine, seen on TV or found on the Internet, and they want to follow up on it. But so often this new piece of intelligence wouldn't fit into their lives and their plans. It's my job to tell them what would. It's also my job to manage people's emotions as well as their money. Every client I've ever had that has made excuses, procrastinated, panicked or got greedy, I've been there to help them do what they needed to do, despite themselves.

FINDING A GOOD FINANCIAL ADVISOR

A good financial advisor has the knowledge and skill to make recommendations specific to your situation, and the patience to be sure you understand the reasoning behind them (although I have to admit, sometimes I talk so fast that clients phone my assistants for a re-explanation).

If you're just starting out or you don't have much money, check with the people at your bank or credit union to see what financial advice they offer. Most of these institutions either have someone on staff or they can point you to someone you can meet with either free or at fairly low rates. You could also try to find a financial advisor who's new to the business and wants to grow with you. Do the record-keeping detailed in Part One and you'll be able to provide a full and accurate snapshot of your current situation, which will save time and give this person an advanced position to start from.

If you have more money and would like your own personal financial advisor, a careful search is in order.

Ellen and Harry

Recently a couple came to me wondering about their cash flow. Harry was retired but still working part-time. Ellen was no longer working, but had only a small pension. Not long before, their advisor had persuaded them to borrow $150,000 to invest in some high-risk real estate ventures—a ski resort, a golf course and commercial real estate. They were lured by the potential big returns and excited because the investments were tax deductible. Besides the various real estate ventures, they still had a nice portfolio of more conservative investments. They wanted to know if there was anything they could do with those investments to increase their return, and therefore their cash flow.

As it turned out, I never even looked at their portfolio. The ski resort and golf course had tanked. They would never get any money out of them, even though they still owed the money they had borrowed to invest. The commercial real estate was yielding a moderate return, but not enough to make up for the two other disastrous leaps they'd taken.

I looked at how much money they owed for the resort and golf course investments, how much Harry was making in his part-time work and how much other money they owed. Just to service the debt, without even tackling much of the principal, they were paying $1,700 a month.

I also looked at their two wish lists. The top item on both was to be out of debt. Probably these high-risk investments had been a last, wild gamble to make themselves self-sufficient—a gamble that had put them further in the soup.

Their salvation was in their life insurance. Years ago they had bought a whole life policy at $400 a month. Along with the $1,700 to service their debt, these folks were spending $2,100 before they even bought food. The cash value on their life insurance policy was $118,000, and to cash it in would not have any serious tax consequences, so I suggested that they cash it in and apply the $118,000 to their $150,000 debt.[1] Their debt was now reduced to a much more manageable $32,000. I asked them to keep paying the $1,700 a month to pay down the remainder of the principal and interest. This would make them debt free within three years. In the meantime, he bought term-to-100 life insurance that would cost them only $100 a month. So there was another $300 a month for cash flow or for debt reduction.

But that's not all. Ellen and Harry had $450,000 in RRSPs. Their original advisor—the one who had sold them on investing in the golf course and ski resort—had advised them to leave that money alone and try to live on Harry's part-time earnings while still paying off their great big debt. But without touching their principal at all, they could get $22,500 a year on only a 5% return. So why not? Then they could move on to the next item on both their wish lists: travel.

Harry and Ellen had an advisor; they just didn't have a very good one. Eventually—and a little too late—they'd figured that out themselves. A good advisor simply doesn't advise a couple nearing retirement to go into debt to invest in high-risk propositions. Maybe if they'd known more when they started looking for a financial advisor they would have chosen someone different.

TRUST, TWO WAYS

You're having trouble in your marriage and thinking about divorce. You'll have to talk to your financial advisor. One of your kids has defaulted on a loan that you co-signed. Your financial advisor will have to know. Your

---

1 This may not work in every case. Whenever you consider cashing in a life insurance policy, if you still require some insurance coverage, make sure you apply for the new insurance and take the medical tests first so you know you're still insurable. Have one insurance policy in place before you consider cancelling another. Always find out what the tax consequences are and how they fit in with your overall situation. Check with your advisor.

sister is executrix of your parents' estate and you think she's mismanaging it. Better talk to your financial advisor.

This person is going to learn some deeply personal details of your life. It had better be someone you can trust, as a person and as a professional.

Ask your friends, family, lawyer and accountant for recommendations. If they recommend someone, ask how long they've been working with this advisor and what this person has done for them. What do they like and not like about the service they've received? Are this person's clients wildly different from you?

While you're in searching mode, collect all your financial information and make it presentable. A financial advisor needs to be fully and truthfully informed in order to help you—the trust has to go both ways. You'll need the record-keeping and calculations from Chapters 2 and 3, along with your tax returns for last year. If you haven't done the work, this is the perfect time to start. Maybe you won't have time to track your spending for a month before you meet a prospective advisor, but you can fill in the annual fixed expenses and monthly income on your Cash Flow Statement (Figure 2.2). Do a quick estimate of your expenses, as well as collecting the details on all your investments. You can also prepare the Personal Balance Sheet (Figure 2.4) and your Wish List. All of this will give a financial advisor a good base to work from.

Qualifications

Financial advisors come from many different fields and bring different types of expertise with them. Some went to school with the intention of becoming Certified Financial Planners, Certified Financial Analysts or Chartered Financial Consultants, but many started off as something else and later earned those certifications. The banking, life insurance, accounting and equities industries also offer their own professional development courses that lead to certification as a financial advisor. (See Appendix 1, page 199) As I write, these certifications all have different names, but in the near future, people from all the different industries will qualify as CFPs, CFAs or CHFCs.

Does it matter if the financial planner you choose is a stockbroker, accountant, banker or underwriter? Not in terms of competence. These are very tough courses, and anyone who has earned such a certification has the knowledge to look at your entire picture and advise you on saving, handling your investments and taxes and planning your estate. What really matters is how your needs mesh with the extra skills your financial planner has to offer.

If you do a lot of investing, you might want someone with a background as a stockbroker or mutual fund representative. If you're self-employed, someone from an accounting background will probably be most helpful. An advisor who is also a lawyer will be able to handle your legal papers. A banker can help when it comes to finding money to borrow. Before you even talk to someone, determine if you'll regularly require some kind of specialized advice or services from a financial planner. If not, your financial advisor will send you to an accountant, lawyer or insurance advisor when the occasion calls for it.

Questions to Ask

Once you've found someone that you think might fit your criteria, it's time to meet and see how you like each other. But what if you've never done this before? How are you going to know, in an hour or so, if this is the person to whom you want to reveal your deepest financial secrets? Yikes! Do the little hairs on your neck stand up? Does this situation remind you of those terrifying first dates?

Sometimes new clients who have been on the hunt for a while come in and tell me about previous encounters: "He spent the whole time telling me about how much money he'd made for his clients." "She kept trying to sell me these gold mining stocks without ever asking me about what I wanted." "Once he knew I only make $40,000 a year, he handed me over to his assistant."

It's the same for me on the receiving end. If somebody comes in and drills me for an hour about my qualifications, experience, attitude, work habits, computer programs, cleaning schedule and office decor, I understand how it feels for clients if someone does that to them.

Most financial planners/advisors/consultants will give you an hour for free. That's great, but your hours are valuable too. Don't waste the opportunity. Before you make an appointment, phone and ask the office staff a few questions that will help you figure out if this relationship is doomed from the start. Eliminate the easy questions that follow and you'll save yourself a lot of time with just a few phone calls:

- What kind of client does this advisor usually handle? If it's mostly CEOs of multinational corporations and you're a postie, you might not be a match.

- How does this person get paid? Financial advisors can be paid by the hour, or receive commissions from buying and selling investments, or be paid through a combination of hourly rates and commissions. Some give you a choice.
- How much does this person charge? If you don't have much money, you may have to go with someone who's just starting out and charging less, or take advantage of the financial advice offered by your bank or credit union.
- Does this person represent any particular company? Some financial advisors are paid by a mutual fund or life insurance company and may try to push that company's products.
- What is this person licensed to buy and sell? Can you afford to pay for the advice to buy a stock or mutual fund and then pay again to actually purchase it?
- What are this person's background and qualifications? Prevent the uncomfortable situation of having to ask the advisor face-to-face by getting the office to tell you. The financial planning associations also have lists of local members and give their qualifications. See Appendix 1 on page 199 for a list of the group names and Web site addresses.
- How long has the advisor been actively doing financial planning? The office will be able to tell you.
- You can ask for client references, but some planners won't want to give you names of other clients. (I'm one of them because I believe in complete client confidentiality.)
- Is this person taking any new clients at the moment?
- How old is this person? If you're nearing retirement you might be more comfortable with an older financial planner, and if you're younger you might prefer someone of the same generation.

First Date

Okay. You've found one or two people who might be right for you. The face-to-face is still a bit nerve-racking, but at least by now you've eliminated the big questions. So what's the drill?

This first encounter is not a contest. In a way, you're courting each other. You're not questioning the person's competence. You're just trying to find out if you're a good fit. You're looking for someone who can understand your situation and work from there. You want to give them enough information to determine if you fit their client profile. You want them to ask enough questions so that they can provide advice tailored to you. You want them to be able to inspire you to do what you need to do. It's the lost art of conversation brought to life again. You talk, they listen. They talk, you listen. Simple, really. While you're there, listen for these warning signs:

- "I get my clients 20% return!" (Uh, 8-10% is a good reliable return. Anything over that involves greater risk. Ask for details. An excellent financial advisor knows that if you're in the stock market, nothing is ever guaranteed.)
- "Look, I got 33% return last year!" (That was last year. Everything's changed since then. Past performance doesn't guarantee future performance, and any financial planner knows that.)
- "I can make you rich. Just leave your finances to me." (Uh oh, I'd kinda like to be involved in the process myself.)

On the other hand, if this person genuinely listens to you and seems to understand your objectives, you might have a match. Here are some questions you should ask:

- Will I be able to meet with you in person one or two times per year?
- What do you think my risk level is?
- Do you understand my personal goals and wishes?
- Will my money be accessible?
- Have you worked with other people in my situation?
- How will you keep me informed?
- Will you send me a summary of the points raised in this meeting, and your approach to them?

If you're not happy with the answers to any of these questions, look around for someone else. This first meeting should fill you with confidence, not make you feel put-upon and uncomfortable. You want someone who's going to work hard to make your wealth grow. There are too many heartbreaking stories of people who trusted this advisor for the wrong reasons and didn't do enough research.

In your hunt for a good financial advisor, you will know you've got a match when you find someone who listens to you, prompts you with questions about your situation, asks for and examines your complete financial information and fully explains any recommendations—potential upside *and* downside. A good advisor will welcome all questions, even if they require a bit of research to answer. Many of my best ideas have come from questions from clients. I may not know the answer, but I can find it and we can learn together.

YOUR RISK PROFILE

Your financial advisor has to understand your need for, or aversion to risk. If you're willing to jump into whatever scheme comes along, you need to be warned about the risk and the actual chances of seeing a return. If you're scared off by the slightest whiff of risk and your savings are losing way to inflation, your financial advisor needs to respect your need to preserve your capital but educate you about other types of investments.

Your risk profile is ruled by two things: what you know and what you feel.

IT *IS* WHAT YOU KNOW

Lots of people blunder in and buy an investment based on a hot tip. Are they doing it because they like taking risks, or because they don't even know they're taking one? Probably the latter. They trust that somebody involved knows what's going on and can make it work.

If you're going to put money into something, find out all you can about it. If you can't understand how it works, don't invest in it. If the person trying to explain it to you can't, don't invest in it. If the people you go to for second, third and fourth opinions can't agree among themselves, or all say it's a gamble, don't invest in it. You just don't know enough about it to get involved. There's nothing wrong with taking a measured risk that's within your financial range, but don't take one without even knowing it's a risk.

It's so easy to be sold a good story. Just remember that the people who tell the good stories are good storytellers. They're good at convincing themselves so they can convince others. Frank Abagnale, author of *Catch Me If You Can,* posed as an airline pilot, a pediatrician, a district attorney and a university professor . . . all before he was 21 years old. (And he'd never even graduated from high school.) He says the lesson he learned is that if you believe in who you say you are, others will believe it too. He's now a consultant to the FBI on fraud.

JACK SCAMS THE GOLF GANG

I had a client who was fooled once. A golfing acquaintance, Jack, told Danny and his group of golf buddies about a resort development that would net some good tax savings. Jack said it was urgent to make a fast decision because so many units were already pre-sold and the whole development would soon be sold out. This place offered a great choice—whoever got in on the ground floor would have a fabulous resort property for the family, or could flip it quickly to make a good profit.

(Oh brother. What a line. Givers are already thinking about the wonderful legacies they can leave their families. Spenders are thinking this might be the one big hit they need to give them all the money they'll ever need. Builders are excited because they're building something. And Savers are seeing all those numbers add up in their heads.)

These golfing friends were already visualizing the glories of the place before one piece of soil had been turned. None had ever been involved in developing a resort before, so they had no idea of the hurdles involved (resorts don't usually make anyone any money until the third buyer). But universally their thought was "Well, we play golf with this guy. He's a member of the club. We'll run into him on the course. He wouldn't lie to us." No risk, right? Once the development started running into trouble, Jack never showed up again.

I'm not saying that every good opportunity is a fraud, just that you should never take anything for granted when it comes to your money. Some of the best ideas in the world have been discussed over a round of golf . . . and some of the worst. Take nothing at face value. And always listen to the part of your body that will tell you if this investment is right for you. Your heart? Your brain? No. Your stomach.

The Tummy Test

We humans come equipped with an amazing piece of warning equipment: the tummy. If your investments are causing you so much worry that you're dyspeptic and can't sleep, they're too risky for you. On the road to retirement, there's something called life. You want to live it to its fullest and not spend the whole time worrying that you're going to lose it all. If you feel the least bit uncomfortable about something, don't invest in it.

Your gut reaction isn't going to tell you whether an investment is a good one or a bad one, just whether or not it's in your particular comfort zone. Strangely enough, your risk profile has little to do with your financial attitude, or any other attitude, for that matter. Lots of Savers have built wonderful stock portfolios, and lots of Spenders keep all their savings in term deposits. I know people who love to leap out of airplanes, but think buying mutual funds is sheer madness. Harry and Ellen got really excited about the three risky investments that nearly blew their savings. It wasn't until they'd lost a bundle that they started to get worried, but even then they were wondering if they could get bigger returns by doing something more aggressive with their conservative stock portfolio.

Everybody has a different comfort level when it comes to financial risk. A friend in the business has observed that people in high-risk occupations are usually happier in low-risk investments such as GICs, while those in stable occupations feel they can afford to take risks because they have an assured income. A stockbroker friend of his told him of a client who was always on the phone asking about her stocks. Finally the broker asked her what she did for a living—turns out she was a prostitute! Knowing this, the broker switched her to GICs and turned a nervous client into a comfortable one.

Your risk level is only one part of the picture for a financial advisor to take into account when suggesting investments. In the next chapter, I'll give a brief rundown of some of the major investment possibilities out there so you'll be able to discuss them with your financial advisor.

HOW TO MAKE YOUR MONEY GROW

When you want to test the depths of a stream, don't use both feet. — Chinese proverb

The good news is that you don't have to save all the money you'll need to retire on. If you did, your working life would be pretty bleak. But the wonderful thing about money is that it grows. From the seeds you've planted, and with some watchful tending, your savings can bear bountiful fruit over the years.

The object is to protect the money you've earned and saved, and add to it the magic of compounding interest. If you invest carefully, you can build wealth over the years. If you invest impulsively, or put off thinking about your financial life until whenever . . . well, your chances of building a secure future are severely diminished.

There are two basic types of investors: loaners and owners.

LOANERS

Savings accounts, bonds, term deposits, GICs, T-bills and mortgages are all called **debt instruments.** You are lending money to an institution for a length of time in return for a promise of interest at the end. Most debt instruments come with guarantees, a fact that appeals to people who don't like any element of the unknown. A lot of Savers prefer to be loaners, as do many people who remember the Depression. For them, any other kind of investment is high risk. But they might be ignoring the risk of falling behind inflation. If inflation is 6% and you're earning 4%, you're still losing money, even though your principal is intact. It's just worth less.

Your standard of living might decrease if you invest in nothing but debt instruments. If you run your Enough numbers and have more than enough, taking inflation into account...fine. You've earned the right to sleep at night. You might not be building up a big pile of interest, but who cares? You're happy. The worst thing you can do is start chasing big gains and undermining your sense of peace.

However, for clients who go to that extreme because they're fearful, I say that everything can disappear, and maybe we should all have vegetable gardens just in case.

Here are some things to think about when you're considering becoming a loaner.

The Lower the Risk, the Lower the Return

Big financial institutions pay less interest than small ones. Government bonds yield less than corporate ones. Short-term deposits pay less interest than long-term ones. It's all been figured out. So if you want to invest in debt instruments and you're willing to accept some negligible risk, you can increase your returns by anywhere from a fraction of a percent to a fraction more than a percent.

Guarantees (some come with a catch)

In Canada, deposits of any kind in financial institutions are insured. A bank will guarantee to cover your money up to $60,000, no matter what happens. A credit union will guarantee anything up to $100,000. If you have a lot of money in GICs and term deposits, think about spreading it among a few institutions to make sure it's completely covered.

Government bonds are backed by the government that sells them. Corporate bonds are one of the first debts a corporation is obligated to pay, even if it goes broke, so, while not absolutely guaranteed, they're pretty reliable. One thing to consider with bonds is the rating. Both governments and corporations are rated on their financial strength, and therefore their ability to pay you back your money. AAA is the top rating and anything below BB is risky. Low-rated bonds are not a good bet for inexperienced investors. The interest goes up as the ratings go down (see above).

Mortgage-backed securities are guaranteed by the federal government— Canada Mortgage and Housing to be exact—if they are held to maturity.

Inflation vs. Interest

Inflation can be both friend and enemy to the loaner. With any investment, your real return is the difference between what you make and what inflation eats up. So if you earned 6% on a bond per year and inflation was 2% a year, your real return was 4% less your income tax. If you're comfortable only with guaranteed investments, the way to get the most out of the interest rates is through using **laddering**. Because long-term rates generally outperform short-term rates, laddering is based on the idea that you want to buy the longest-term deposits or GICs. Start by buying one each of a one-year, two-year, three-year, four-year and five-year deposit. When the one-year is up, convert it to a five-year. Eventually, you will have all five-year deposits, with one coming up for renewal every year. This way you will average out the interest rates and you'll still have the benefit of the higher interest rates that result from the longer term. (Every once in a while there is an inverted-yield curve, which means that short-term deposits are worth more than long-term. Don't worry about it. This situation never lasts long.)

When is a Bond Not a Bond?

If one bond is good, then a whole bunch must be better, right? Sorry. It's a misconception out there that a bond mutual fund is safer than one bond.

When you buy a bond at 6% interest and hold it to maturity, you're guaranteed that your principal will be returned to you plus the interest on the bond. If you sell that bond on the open market before the maturity date, and the interest rate is lower than 6% that day, you'll make money because your bond guarantees a higher rate of return than the current interest rate. If the interest rate is higher than 6% the day you sell the bond, you'll lose money.

Bond funds don't buy bonds and hold them to maturity. They use bonds as commodities to buy and sell on the open market. These funds are just as volatile as stocks because they are at the mercy of interest rates. For example, if you have a +1% interest rate hike, a bond fund can have a –3% return for the year. On the other hand, if interest rates are high and are dropping, a bond fund can have a tremendous return. So a bond mutual fund can still present a lot of risk and opportunity.

If you buy a bond fund you're also paying an annual management fee. But why pay a fund manager to do what you can do yourself? You can buy bonds themselves for a very small one-time fee. If you don't like risk, you're better off just to buy a bond and keep it.

Tax Bite on Interest

When you're planning your investment strategy, keep in mind that the interest you earn as a loaner is taxed at a higher rate than the capital gains you earn as an owner. That's something else to calculate when you're deciding whether or not to put your money in a term deposit or bond. Will the interest beat inflation and if it does, will it still beat inflation once you've paid the tax on it? At the time of writing, 100% of the interest is added to your income, but only a percentage of your capital gains or dividends is added to your income. That's a good reason to hold debt instruments in your RRSPs and other kinds of investments outside.

Locked or Not

The less access you have to your money, the higher the interest it will earn, as a rule. The financial institutions lend out your money if they know you have committed your money for a long period of time. They know they can charge more for it because they'll have your money for longer. They can afford to pay more for it. Most investors are both owners and loaners so they always have some principal that's protected. If you remember 1998 when the Asian economies collapsed and sank the rest of the world's stock markets at the same time, you'll understand why this is a good idea. Especially if you are about to retire, buy a home, or take your world cruise, you might want some of your cash readily available instead of having to sell some of your stocks at their lowest value. Your age or stage of life and your own needs dictate how much liquidity you'll require in your investment portfolio. More on ages and stages in Chapter 10.

OWNERS

As an owner, your fortunes rise and fall with the success of the enterprise or property you've invested in, and with the market forces that affect it. You have no guarantee that you will make money, and no guarantee that you'll keep the money you started with. You're the last one to get paid. The market isn't mathematically perfect, so stock in a perfectly good company with perfectly respectable profits might head down, while stock in something with no track record, millions of dollars in debt and paltry earnings might spike. We saw the situation just recently, when young Internet companies seemed to corner the market while anything that wasn't high-tech might as well have disappeared. It was a mania, and one that eventually corrected itself, as they all do.

There's no predicting, and yet every day millions of North Americans trade stocks, buy into mutual funds, spend money on art, invest in real estate and purchase commodities. Are all of these folks danger-loving wackos? Not at all. Almost half of all Canadians now own stocks, either on their own or through mutual funds. The potential rewards of owning are so much greater than those of loaning that they're willing to take the chance. On top of that, any growth on these investments, called capital gains, is taxed at a lower rate than interest (unless they're held in RRSPs).

Although there are no guarantees, not all of these investments are equally risky either. Buying stock every month in a blue-chip company that pays a dividend, or putting your money regularly into a good-quality stock mutual fund is hardly diving off a cliff. Lots of owner-type investments carry little risk at all. Others can be money graveyards.

THREE REWARDING INVESTMENT STRATEGIES

No one's going to make you wealthy. You're going to make yourself wealthy by spending less than you want to, or making more than you need to and putting away a percentage of your earnings whether you want to or not. That's the real hard work of getting Enough. If you invest as an owner, you might make a few big hits, which you can consider bonuses. In all likelihood, your portfolio will also make good money on top of inflation. If you put away money regularly, over time it will accumulate and build. Steady, steady, steady. Boring, boring, boring. But it works.

I can't tell you which stocks will spike or which mutual funds will grow exponentially. Wish I could. This would be a much shorter book and I'd have a lot more free time. No investment is ever guaranteed to leave you better off than when you put money in. The only piece of blanket advice I can give you is don't follow blanket advice. That said, I'll tell you some things I've learned and observed over the last couple of decades.

Strategy One: Invest, Don't Speculate

There's a difference between speculating and investing. Investing is for the long term. It's done regularly and it's done with a respect for the underlying value of a company, fund or property being invested in. Speculating is gambling. It's betting on a short-term gain and, if that happens, grabbing the profit and getting out. It's hoping that the stock you bought for 35¢ will spring up to 85¢ in a week. Speculating requires a whole lot of energy and attention, because you have to get in and get out. But many of my clients who never check their investments from one year to the next have been more successful than the smash-and-grab investors. It's time in the market rather than timing the market that wins in the long run. Putting your money in a mutual fund and leaving it there is a good example of how this works. If you look at the charts they send out in their annual reports ("$10,000 invested in 1978 is now worth . . .") you can see how even mediocre funds make money over time. The same is true of solid stocks.

Investing for the long term also saves the expense of buying and selling. Even if you're only paying $7 to buy or sell your stocks each time, it can add up if you're jumping in and out of things all the time. And if you're paying a stockbroker a percentage of each transaction—yow. It usually costs money to move in and out of different mutual funds too. So relax! Let your money make money and leave it alone.

If you crave the thrill of speculation, do it with your fun money—money that your other investments have made for you and you didn't have to earn. That way you can have the excitement—and maybe some big gains—without risking your principal. Don't borrow or buy on margin; that way, if you lose the money, at least you don't owe it.

Strategy Two: Dollar Cost Average

Buy Low, Sell High: the law of investing. Okay, fine, but how many people have actually succeeded in doing that? Market timing isn't an exact science. If it were, stockbrokers would work for one month and retire. Dollar cost averaging takes advantage of the ups and downs of the markets without a lot of work on your part. You choose a few good stocks and/or mutual funds. You buy every month, come what may. When the market is up you're buying fewer shares; when the price drops you're getting more for your money. Meantime the stock or mutual fund keeps going up on average. Over time the dollar cost averages out.

I like this approach because not only is it rewarding financially, it's also easy on the emotions. You can only do this with solid companies and mutual funds, so it's unlikely you'll lose everything. Even during market corrections, reliable investments lose only 30 to 40% of their value, and then head back up again. Meanwhile, because you're not concerned with the day-to-day price changes, you can sleep at night. If you're paying attention at all, you might even be rooting for the occasional dip so that you can stock up.

Strategy Three: Diversify

Remember what your mom said about not putting all your eggs in one basket? She was giving you investment advice, clever woman. Stock markets run on emotion. Whole sectors explode and then fade out. Today's star is tomorrow's black hole. And because only a small portion of the change is based on what the companies are actually accomplishing, nobody knows when one sector is going to explode or fade out. That's why you have to diversify your portfolio. Different countries, different industries, different types of investments don't all do well at the same time. But usually over time they will average out. I compare a balanced portfolio to a teeter-totter. One side will be up and the other side down, but there is always movement as well as balance.

If you only have a few dollars to invest, the best way to diversify is to buy a selection of mutual funds. Each mutual fund already contains a number of stocks, and buying funds in several sectors insures even further variation. Check the contents of each mutual fund to make sure there's not a lot of duplication. There's no use owning two funds if they both hold largely the same stocks. I recommend having no more than 12 funds, and if you're starting out, keep it to three or four.

If you have more money to invest, it's time to talk about true diversification, beyond mutual funds. This might be real estate, mortgages, art or gold. As you have more and more money, this kind of diversification becomes necessary, because you never know what's going to happen. Inflation, market corrections, deflation, world catastrophes—each of these can be good for some investments and bad for others.

There are many ways to get to Enough. Some people have more affinity for one vehicle than another, as they would for one vocation or another. If you have something that works for you, go for it. But I do know that these three strategies will work, and they'll work for the average person as well as the wealthy person. There's lots of room for error, but you won't succumb to a fatal flaw.

OWNER INVESTMENTS: THE BASICS

I'm not going to go into every single owner investment possibility here because that's another whole book—and I think it's already been written several times. What I will do is talk in general about owner strategies that work for most investors. If you want more details, ask your financial advisor.

Your Own Home

Owning your own home is the holy grail of owner investing. If you've read to this point, you've probably realized that I'm a big believer in owning your own home. Having a roof over your head (that you can afford) gives a terrific sense of security and builds in value at the same time. Once the mortgage is paid off, you will have that much more money that you can spend or invest every month.

DON'T BUY IN A MARKET FRENZY

If you're buying a home, there are a few things to remember. Don't buy during a market frenzy. Both Toronto and Vancouver have recently undergone periods of wildly escalating house prices. After a couple of years, prices came down again. How do you know a market frenzy? You'll keep hearing the phrase "If you don't get in now you'll never be able to afford it."

DON'T TAKE IT TO THE LIMIT

When you're buying a home, don't go to the limit of what you can afford. Remember that when you're buying, there will be transaction costs, legal costs, property transfer tax, inspection reports, and sometimes you're paying part of the year's property taxes. Those one-time expenses should be included in your calculations for whatever down payment you can afford. From that, figure out what you can afford to spend in mortgage payments every month. Leave some wiggle room. Mortgage rates need to be renegotiated after a certain time. If they go up and you can barely afford your current mortgage, you could be in trouble. Some major expense could also come along and broadside you if you haven't planned for the unexpected. If you take all of this into account and discover you really can't afford the house you want just yet, you might consider buying in a cheaper neighbourhood, building some equity and then moving on from there, or purchasing a fixer-upper in the neighbourhood where you want to live and doing renovations over time.

Is it forever or just for now?

When you buy a home, will you want to live there forever? This is an important question to ask. If you plan to sell it so you can move up to your dream home, any renovations will have to be made with an eye to the market. Some years, the bathroom Jacuzzi is what everybody wants; sometimes it's a rainfall shower. If you plan to sell your home so that you can move up a step, make it desirable to the general market. Don't put in all sorts of quirky details that buyers might not want. Read the magazines and check with the contractors to see what's desirable now.

If you plan to live there forever (like the millionaire next door), then feel free to make the changes you want. Just make them within your budget.

A house is the biggest and safest investment most people will ever make. There are other real estate investments: real estate investment trusts, residential and commercial real estate investments and property development. I'll talk about them later in this chapter.

Mutual Funds

When you buy into a mutual fund, you're buying shares in a company that exists to invest money. Where you might be able to afford five to 10 stocks, securities or other investments, a mutual fund will trade in 30 to 50 or more, so if some lose value the rest should make up for it over time. Most of these companies offer a range of funds, with different levels of risk and different specializations. Banks and credit unions have also introduced their own lines of mutual funds to take advantage of their customers' desire to kick it up a notch.

For most of us who want to go beyond term deposits, mutual funds are the easiest type of investment because we don't have to watch and manage them all the time. A fund manager is doing that. That's not to say that mutual funds always make money. But even with market ups and downs, over time most mutual funds make money grow faster than debt instruments.

Mutual fund definitions

Hoo, boy. Mutual funds are getting more and more involved all the time, with new kinds of funds popping up every day. If you want to know about them all, talk to your financial advisor. The following definitions are based on how fund managers build their portfolios.

Balanced: These funds attempt to have a balanced portfolio of term deposits, blue chip stocks and a few aggressive stocks. As a rule, they're in the middle of the pack as far as earnings. On the other hand, they tend to stand up well to the more aggressive funds during market corrections because they're conservative. I personally don't care for them because they contain bonds and that means you're paying part of your management fee every year for something you could have bought and held yourself.

Growth (also called Equities): These are more aggressive funds. Their managers look for companies with the potential to make a big profit. Some growth funds are diversified, and others concentrate their efforts in one sector, like telecommunications, finance or mining. These funds tend to go up and down with the sector. Generally, the more specialized the fund, the more volatile the fund.

Top down: The managers of top-down funds analyze the big picture first: what is happening in the economy right now and what sectors are likely to experience upturns. Then they buy leading stocks in those sectors to represent them in their portfolios, while still maintaining a balance from other sectors.

Momentum: The managers of momentum funds look for upward trends in specific stocks or whole sectors, invest there, then try to predict the peak so they can get out and do it again.

Sector rotation: This is the more aggressive form of top-down management. The managers look for the next hot sectors, invest heavily in them, and then move out of them to what they believe are the upcoming hot sectors. These funds hope to get in on the next big trend before it becomes a trend.

Bottom up: Bottom-up fund managers look for companies with strong fundamentals and analyze those companies thoroughly before they buy shares in the companies.

Value: Value fund managers seek out stocks they believe are undervalued despite good performance. The hope is that the stock price will one day be more in line with the true worth of the companies.

Index funds: Index funds reflect the mix of companies on different stock exchanges. Some mirror as closely as possible the stocks on an exchange; others buy the same percentages in various sectors but try to choose only the better companies.

If you bought a fund based on NASDAQ in 1998, you would have done spectacularly well until about mid-2000, but if you'd bought one based on the Japanese stock market, Nikkei, you would have lost some ground. These funds don't require much management, so the management fees are lower.

Exchange-traded funds (ETFs): ETFs are index funds that are bought and sold in the same way as stocks. Because they're traded on a stock exchange, they're cheaper to buy, especially if you buy through an on-line broker.

Labour-sponsored venture capital corporations: LSVCCs are investment funds sponsored by labour to provide capital for small- to medium-sized businesses. The purpose is to create and protect jobs by investing in companies based in the province, to provide economic growth and diversification of the provincial economy and to increase the supply of venture capital. Fifteen to 20% of your investment is eligible for federal and provincial tax credits. Think of these as long-term investments. You have to be in them for several years, so your money isn't liquid. If you're looking for short-term or income generating investments, these aren't for you. And even though some of them have done extremely well, remember that they're very speculative in nature.

Segregated funds: These funds, sold by life insurance companies, have two distinctive benefits. When you buy a segregated fund, you're paying a little bit more for management and your fund is insured. After 10 years, you're guaranteed to get your principal back, even if the fund has dropped, or if you die, your estate gets the principal. If the fund does better, of course, you or your estate will receive the extra as well.

Another advantage is that if you name a preferred beneficiary (spouse, parents or children), segregated funds are creditor-proof. This is a great advantage if you're in business for yourself and putting everything on the line. I've had many situations where segregated funds protected a family who would have lost everything. One of my clients, an engineer, had his own company which depended entirely on him. He was the brains of the business. When he died suddenly, the bank forced the sale of the business and it sold for about 10¢ on the dollar because it wasn't worth as much without him. The bank then came after the family for everything the business still owed, but the segregated funds couldn't be touched. Many times this is the only money the family has left.

Unfortunately, the only creditor these funds can't protect you from is Canada Customs and Revenue Agency. CCRA can't force you to cash the funds, but they can put a lien on them when you do. If you owe taxes, however, this will at least give you time to negotiate.

How to buy

It's tempting to buy a mutual fund that has performed spectacularly for a couple of years. But what that really means is that you'll be paying a higher price for your shares and the fund is probably headed for a correction soon. A mutual fund that did exceptionally well last year might not win any prizes this year, and one that's been chugging along quietly might suddenly be in a hot sector and see its earnings zoom.

Buying your mutual funds by *only* looking back is like driving by only looking in the rearview mirror. But although you shouldn't use past performance to predict future performance, looking backwards when you want to buy a mutual fund has some validity. It does give you the big picture of a fund's or manager's performance. You want a fund manager who has a good track record over 10 years. Generally speaking, most fund managers have had one terrific year, two above average, two good years, and sometimes two bad years in that time. No one calls it right all the time. Allow for the odd bad year and don't panic. Even with those, a mutual fund is likely to make money in the long run. If it's outperforming inflation and making a bit more, that's what you're looking for. Stay away from funds that have consistently underperformed the comparable funds. Newspaper listings rank funds within their categories, so it's easy to see which ones are lagging behind.

If you're a new investor, buying the funds that have just corrected is a good way to go. You may have to be patient, but eventually they'll hit again. In 1997, Canadian equity funds were in the tank and could be bought very cheaply. Three years later they performed very well.

What you pay

When you buy a mutual fund there are some expenses involved.

MER: The Management Expense Ratio can range from 1.5 to 3%—this is the hidden annual cost in a mutual fund that goes to paying commissions, management, overhead and other costs. When the newspapers track the mutual funds, it's with the MER taken out already. All mutual funds have MERs.

No-load: All you pay is the MER. Some funds sell direct to the public, and all administration costs come out of the MER. Some financial advisors sell no-load funds, and their commissions come out of the MER or they charge an hourly fee or a percentage of your portfolio.

Front-end load: The fee is paid up front, usually from 1% to 5%. For example, if you pay $10,000 into a mutual fund, and the front-end load is 3%, the 3% is taken off your investment, so you've actually bought $9,700 worth of funds. If the fund earned 10% that year, you would have made $970, not $1,000.

Back end load: Your full $10,000 is invested in the mutual fund, but there's a penalty if you withdraw your money before six to seven years. There's a decreasing percentage over the six to seven years, so the longer you have the fund the less the penalty. Mutual fund companies will often let you move from fund to fund within their family of funds without a penalty.

Distributions: Normally mutual funds buy and hold stocks. But when a fund manager has sold stock through the year and has made money, the money is distributed among the units, and that's considered a capital gain. You as a unitholder must pay your share of the capital gains unless the fund is in your RRSP. If you buy a fund and get a distribution shortly afterwards, you'll have to pay capital gains tax on earnings you didn't share. When you're shopping for the right mutual fund, ask your financial advisor to find out if there's a big distribution coming up, and then buy afterwards.

TAXES ON DISTRIBUTIONS

Beware of doubling up on the taxes you pay on mutual fund distributions. Sometimes you'll get a T-3 slip from a mutual fund that you own, even though you didn't sell any units. That's a distribution (see above) and you have to pay capital gains tax on it. Keep your T-3s and statements so you'll have a record of how much tax you've paid. No one else will.

The original price you paid for your mutual fund is called the Adjusted Cost Base (ACB). When you sell your fund, the difference between that original cost and what you sold it for is your taxable capital gain. But you've already paid tax on the distributions. Add the T-3s to the original cost. Now your ACB will be the price of your units after the last distribution rather than what you paid originally. This is particularly important if you've transferred the funds from one institution to another.

By the time you read this book, there will probably be dozens of new mutual fund products and ways of investing. There are always exciting things coming, and some are genuinely new and present fresh opportunities. Just remember to look at them closely before you discard what you have.

Stocks

I'm not going to talk in detail about the stock market because it's such a long and complicated subject. Warrants, puts, calls, stock options, IPOs, small and large cap stocks—it's like learning a new language. If you want to learn more, there are many books on the subject. One I can recommend is *The Only Investment Guide You'll Ever Need* by Andrew Tobias. Instead, some observations.

When you buy stock, you become a part-owner of a company that is producing goods or providing services. As an owner, you participate in the profits of the company as the stock price rises. Many blue-chip companies also pay dividends—which are a percentage of the profits—to shareholders. You are, however, the last to get paid. As the profits go up, your stocks should be worth more, but don't count on it. The market is not always rational.

For that reason, I don't manage clients' individual stocks. I ask people to use a stockbroker, because I have a strong need to be liked, and people are often mad at their stockbrokers. Stockbrokers might suggest an investment because it's got good, solid credentials or it's in a hot sector or everybody else is recommending it, but none of that really means much because the stock market runs on emotion and rumour. If the stock takes a beating, it's not necessarily the stockbroker's fault. It's probably the fault of the rest of the investing world. I guess that's what makes stocks so exciting for people who love taking risks.

The risk alters with the sector, size and type of company, but in general, the shorter your time horizon, the greater the volatility. It's the difference between a long-distance and a close-up view. If you climb a mountain, you experience every tree, rock, dip and hummock. If you look at the mountain from far away, you see the slope. Imagine if you'd bought Microsoft in the eighties, when it had already established itself as the industry leader in software. Imagine if you'd kept investing. There may have been the odd dip, but on the whole it would have headed upwards. Even the antitrust suit, with its serious road burn, wouldn't have taken away from the stock's phenomenal performance overall.

Part of the gamble of buying stocks is that every now and then a new idea will come along that wipes out the old ones. Or a company will come out of nowhere with something revolutionary, and on its heels will come a mania. Or, for some reason that no one can fathom, one sector will suddenly become sexy.

The market has seen lots of manias. In the early 1900s, there were hundreds of oil companies drilling everywhere. Some of those stocks are today's Exxon-Mobils. Most are wallpaper. The same is true of the dot.coms of the late nineties. A few are still with us. A lot blew everything on 1999 Superbowl commercials and died shortly afterwards. As an individual investor, you have scant access to the information that might indicate what the next mania is going to be (or you have access to so much information that you have no way of sorting through it all). That's why I suggest that you invest in solid companies with good track records and prospects for the future. Stay in them and invest regularly. Otherwise you'll be led by your emotions.

DOES THIS SOUND FAMILIAR?

- "Whoa, look at that stock go. It's gotta be near the top!"
- "Whoa, that thing's still going. I'd better borrow money to buy some."
- "Whoa, I've made 20% profit in two months. But I'm not gonna sell. If it keeps going like this, I'm rich."
- "Whoa, it's taken a big hit. I'd better sell before it goes down some more."
- "Whoa, I'd better find a good quick hit so I can pay off my margin call on the last one."

It's the sad, but common tale of the small investor. Our friend was speculating rather than investing, and did several things wrong:

- Bought high—watched the stock rise and rise and believed it would keep rising forever
- Bought on margin—borrowed money to speculate
- Didn't take a profit—assumed the stock would keep going up forever
- Sold low—panicked when the stock fell
- Had to make up a loss—didn't have enough to cover what was borrowed, now wants to make it up by gambling some more.

By reacting so predictably, our friend has just fuelled a stock market mania and helped make a few wiser heads a bit richer. If you're a short-term investor looking for quick profits, set your profit limits and sell when you hit them.

When I first got into the business, an old moneylender told me "You'll never go broke taking a profit." It was great advice. I never forgot it. Don't get greedy, and don't look back. Buying and selling stocks can be an enjoyable game for people who are willing to take the time and effort involved in understanding the process and who can manage their emotions as they play.

My clients who have made the really big wins in the stock market are the ones with stock options, because they know the company and are working to make the company grow. Stock options in a company give employees the right to buy shares at a set price within a certain time frame. If the price goes up, they can still buy at the set price, then immediately flip for a profit. If the price goes down, they don't have to buy. If you know the company and the people in the company, or even if you know the field and have access to the people in it, trust yourself. Buy on a regular basis as well. You might do better than average. Just don't bet everything. For the rest of us, slow and steady will win the race. And if you really, really crave some excitement in your portfolio, go crazy with 10% of it. You can have your thrills, but you won't be betting the farm.

WRAP ACCOUNTS

These are not investments in themselves, but a way of pulling all your investments together under one umbrella with professional management. Rather than paying a commission on each transaction, you pay an annual management fee from 0.5 to 3% of the value of your portfolio. The more the portfolio is worth, the smaller the percentage. You need a substantial amount of money to get into a wrap account—$50,000 at least. Some companies require at least $100,000 to $150,000. Unlike mutual fund management fees, a wrap account administration fee is tax deductible.

Art and Other Valuables

Generally, unless you're a dealer in such things, art, jewelry and antiques are not investments. They can be. They hold their value and increase. But usually people buy them for the love of the things themselves. If they buy hoping to make a profit, they'd better know what they're doing. For example, one of my clients was sold on a sculptor whose works' value kept going up. The artist and the dealer guaranteed that they would buy back any piece at the price the client bought it for. He invested a lot of money in the artist's work, to the exclusion of all others (and believe me, I was in there advising him to diversify). Somehow, when it came time to sell a piece or two, he couldn't—nor would the artist or the dealer buy them back. Now he has to live with his collection and hope that the artist will become famous someday. Be careful of guarantees. The only thing that is truly guaranteed is a fully insured GIC.

If you love first editions, silver art deco cigarette cases or English watercolours, that's fine. Buy them and enjoy them. Make that your reason to buy, and don't consider them an investment. Most people never sell these things anyway.

REAL ESTATE INVESTING

I've always had a fondness for real estate. But I warn you, even if it's real, it can still be an illusion. The principle I always followed was this: if everything that could go wrong does go wrong, will I still break even? If the pipes burst, the contractor doesn't pay anybody, the roof needs fixing and I can't find a tenant for two months, will I be able to carry the costs without getting into financial difficulty? If so, I can afford this investment.

A lot of people buy real estate thinking that the market will just keep going up and up. Generally I don't count on the market to make money for me on real estate. I do something to increase the value of the property by adding on or updating (currently people are looking for great bathrooms and kitchens), and I try to improve its value in such a way that even if the market drops, I will get back my original price and all I will lose is my own time and effort. One good thing is that usually everything doesn't go wrong at the same time.

Real estate is not infallible. The old saying "Buy real estate: they're not making any more of it" is true for some places—Toronto for example, as the financial centre of Canada, attracts more and more people all the time. Vancouver is hemmed in by mountains and sea and doesn't have many places to expand. But many other cities and towns are losing people or not growing, so prices are stagnant or falling. The other old saying, "Location, location, location" is more in tune with the reality of real estate today. And I'll add a new one: "Timing, timing, timing."

MORTGAGES

Holding someone else's mortgage is low risk in all but the hairiest real estate markets because you have the property itself as equity. If the mortgagee defaults, the registered mortgage holders are left with the building.

You might have to hold onto it until you are able to sell the property. In the meantime, you can probably get rental income from the property. You have to be a pretty sophisticated investor to be holding mortgages on your own.

REAL ESTATE INVESTMENT TRUSTS (REITs)

REITs consolidate the assets of many real-estate investors in an investment vehicle that's more liquid than real estate itself. Income-producing properties are the backbone, rather than real estate development. Some REITs hold the properties themselves, others buy shares in companies that own properties.

Because they're based on long-term leases, the REITs that actually own the properties are reasonably secure. They're not infallible however. Some have thin trade volume, which means you might not be able to get out when you want to. Some own a lot of properties that they picked up cheaply because no one else wanted them. Look at the underlying value, the properties inside the REIT, before you buy.

The REITs that hold shares instead of properties are more subject to market fluctuations. They can have bigger gains, but bigger losses too.

REAL ESTATE DEVELOPMENT

Leave real estate development to the pros. Most of them have already lost their shirts a few times and they know what can go wrong. Real estate development is no place for the small investor, no matter how foolproof the glossy brochures and 3-D computer graphics make it seem. If you don't have money to spare, don't get in on the ground floor of a real estate development.

TAX SHELTERS

When you invest in a tax shelter, you can write off some of it against income you've earned. The government creates tax shelters when it's motivated to stimulate the economy in a certain sector.

Remember MURBs back in the eighties? Multiple Unit Residential Buildings. The government wanted to stimulate housing starts. Once there was a tax saving involved, real estate prices went up. People forgot to look at the underlying value of the properties and overpaid. When prices dropped, they lost money. Another tax saving—only one they didn't want. Investment in the Canadian film industry was also a tax shelter for a while and people were putting their money into cheesy B-movies that never saw a screen.

Never be motivated by tax savings alone. The investment has to be sound. Then if you have tax savings, it's a bonus.

SOME RULES FOR INVESTING

There are no rules for getting rich quick. However, there are rules for getting rich slow. Keep these in mind as you go about investing for your future.

- Diversify your portfolio.
- Invest regularly for dollar cost averaging.
- Hold for the long term.
- Anything that becomes a mania will eventually become overpriced and drop in value.
- Buy quality.
- Don't panic when the price falls—you'll only lose money if you sell.
- Nobody ever went broke taking a profit.
- If you want to speculate, do it with 10% of your portfolio.
- No one's going to care about your money as much as you do, so pay attention.
- If you can't understand it, don't invest in it.
- Don't be pushed into investing in something—there will always be opportunities.
- If the person who's trying to explain it to you can't, that person doesn't understand it either.
- Don't beat yourself up over what you should have done.
- Don't borrow money to speculate.
- If you lose sleep over it, it's too high risk for you.
- If it looks too good to be true, it probably is.
- If you need help, get a financial advisor.

If you do everything using this conservative program, you'll do fine. Keep investing. Buy quality, buy consistently. When one does very well, you might go back and reconfigure them a bit. It isn't exciting, but it works.

Find the risk level that works for you. If you want the guarantees of term deposits and you've reached your Enough number, fine. Sometimes when people are relaxed about having enough they're more relaxed about the fun money they have and they let themselves risk a bit more and often make more money—they know they're not going to end up on the streets.

If you want those bigger profits, invest (carefully) in the stock market. Go for good companies, index funds or high-quality mutual funds. If you like risk, play with 10% of your portfolio and keep the rest in solid owner-investments. Just know that you won't hit it big all the time, and you will see some losses along the way. But if you don't panic you'll be okay. A good stockbroker or financial planner can help you invest sensibly.

All of this (rather dry) information is offered to give you a foundation—and only a foundation. There's a whole continuum of investment possibilities. Some are right for you. But there's much more to know about each of them. If you're going to make your money grow, you need to have a working knowledge of what's out there. What I've tried to do here is to give you a basic vocabulary so that you can get more out of your conversations with your bank, stockbroker, financial advisor or accountant.

In the next chapter we'll look at the most valuable investment tools available to Canadians. And believe it or not, they come from the government.

CHAPTER

REGISTERED PLANS

*Each of us has the choice—we must work for the money
or we must make the money work for us.* — *Conrad Leslie*

In Canada we have a couple of wonderful shelters for our savings: RRSPs
for you and RESPs for your kids. Both of them allow your contributions
to grow without being taxed until they are used. But, being products of a
government bureaucracy, they are not perfectly straightforward.

While in general everyone should take advantage of every possible
cent that can be saved, tax deferred or within an RRSP or RESP, there are
exceptions. I find that a lot of people make mistakes because they pick up
an idea from the media and apply it without first understanding it. "I
heard it was really a good idea to start RRSPs for your children. . ."
Maybe, but not at the expense of your own. "I read that you can use your
RRSP money to buy a house . . ." Maybe, but you're in a low tax bracket right now, so you're better off to save for a house outside your RRSP.
Bits of information can be useful, but unless you can put them into the
context of your entire financial situation, they can kneecap you.

I'll try to take care of those maybes by giving you a fundamental
understanding of the purpose of each kind of saving program.

REGISTERED RETIREMENT SAVINGS PLANS

When you have money to sock away you have two choices: RRSP or non-
RRSP. Both of them have their advantages, and as I take you through the
basics, the advantages will become clear.

In an RRSP, you can put a certain percentage of your earnings away now, and you won't be charged tax on it or the money it earns until you collect it later as income. This reduces your taxable income and frees up more money to save. Let's say that you're in a 40% tax bracket. If you have $2,000 and you don't put it in an RRSP, you pay 40% to Canada Customs and Revenue Agency and you're left with only $1,200 to invest. If you put it in an RRSP, the entire $2,000 will grow and compound: you're earning interest on the $1,200 plus the $800 that CCRA would have had in its coffers. As you can see in Figure 8.1, even at a mere 6% annual return, putting the money in your RRSP doubles your accumulated savings in just 15 years.

Figure 8.1: **Accumulated Savings Inside and Outside an RRSP**

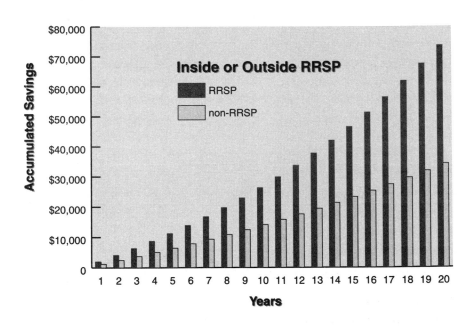

Your RRSP will earn interest and compound, tax free, until you withdraw the money (normally when you retire). Initially the theory was that when you retired you would be in a lower tax bracket and would be paying lower taxes. But I hope you amass so much that you'll be in the same tax bracket when you retire as when you worked! If you do end up in the same tax bracket, you'll still enjoy the compounding effect on a lot of money you otherwise would have paid to CCRA back when you were saving.

One of the best things you can do for your retirement is just to keep adding money and having it compound. If you take money out of your RRSP before you retire, that money will be added to your taxable income for the year, meaning you'll pay extra tax that year. That's a big price to pay, and that's what makes an RRSP such a fantastic forced savings program, even for Givers, Builders and Spenders who have trouble saving.

What is Eligible?

Your RRSP contribution limit is calculated on last year's income plus any unused RRSP room from previous years (called a carry-forward). You can use income earned from these sources to calculate your RRSP contribution limit:

- Salary
- Self-employed income after expenses
- Rental property income
- Royalties
- Employment Insurance.

You *cannot* calculate your RRSP contribution limit using income earned from these sources:

- Canada Pension
- Old Age Security
- Tax-free disability pensions
- Workers' Compensation
- Interest, dividends or capital gains from investments.

At the moment, you can contribute 18% of your eligible income from the previous year, to a maximum of $13,500. If you are part of a pension plan at work, your contribution and your employer's contribution (called your Pension Adjustment Number) are subtracted from the 18%. These figures might change. In any case, CCRA calculates it for you. You will see how much contribution room you have when you get your Notice of Assessment back after you've filed your income tax return.

When You Shouldn't Contribute to Your RRSP

Alex and Meagan are young, employed and saving to buy their first home. They figure the best thing would be to put their savings in RRSPs, because they know they can borrow up to $20,000 from their RRSPs to pay for a home, and the tax break will give them more money to save. They're pretty pleased with themselves.

But hang on. Much as I rail on about maxing out your RRSPs, there are two situations when that's exactly what you shouldn't do.

1. LOW INCOME, HIGH EXPECTATIONS

Meagan and Alex are just starting their careers and aren't making much money yet. In a few years they expect to see some quantum leaps in income. As they advance in their careers and start making more, they'll be taxed at a higher and higher percentage of their income. In all likelihood, they'll never see a tax bracket again this low. The tax break they'll get from contributing to their RRSP is not that significant right now.

Will they lose their RRSP room if they don't use it? No. In fact, the RRSP contribution room can accumulate from year to year. This provision is called carry-forward, *i.e.*, you can carry forward all of your unused contribution room into later years.

There's no time limit on the carry-forward. From the first time you file an income tax return, you can build up eligible contribution room for as many years as you want and use it whenever you want. So if you're looking at making more money down the road, you'll reap big benefits then if you don't max out your RRSP now.

A caution, though: if you're in a low tax bracket now and recognize that you'll only make the regular, steady increases in salary that come with your job, you should definitely take advantage of whatever RRSP contribution room you have. The tax break, however small, will give you more money to save, and you'll need everything you can to put away for when you retire.

2. SAVING FOR SOMETHING BIG

There's another good reason for Alex and Meagan not to make RRSP contributions at this point: they're trying to save $20,000 toward their first home. If they save that money within their RRSPs, then take it out to use as a down payment, they'll have to put the money back into their RRSPs at a certain percentage per year over the next 15 years. If they miss a year's portion of the payback, that amount will be added to their taxable income for the year, possibly boosting them to a higher tax bracket.

So now they're paying a mortgage, they have hardly any retirement savings, they have to pay all that money back into their own RRSPs over the next 15 years and they've lost the compounding effect of what was in there before. They may not have any money left over to make their regular RRSP contributions, which means they won't receive the tax benefits of contributing. No, no, no! These folks have left themselves no wiggle room, especially if they're buying at the outer limit of what they can afford. They're house poor. If an unexpected baby comes along, or a sickness or a downturn in the economy, they have no resources to fall back on.

Here's a better way. Meagan and Alex don't contribute to their RRSPs for three or four years while they save like crazy (she's a Saver, he's a Builder). When they've finally saved $20,000, they plunk it down on a home. Now they've got a mortgage, but with whatever's left over they can start contributing to their RRSPs and saving toward retirement. They've also built up significant carry-forward room, so in a few years when they can afford to put more in their RRSPs, they'll be able to catch up. And they can use the tax refunds from contributing to their RRSPs to reduce their mortgage even further.

Alex and Meagan can achieve their down payment even faster if they have the discipline to live on one salary. If they do that without contributing to their RRSPs, they'll be able to build up a hefty down payment in just a few years, which will make their mortgage easier to handle. They might even have some left over to catch up on their RRSPs once they've bought their home.

This kind of discipline comes more easily to Savers and Builders than to Givers and Spenders. For a lot of them, RRSPs are the only way they can save anything. The tax refund is the carrot and the extra tax if they raid their RRSPs is the stick. If RRSPs are the only way you can save, so be it. But if you can apply some of the saving techniques from Chapter 5, there are times when saving outside your RRSP is a better way. Some situations are not as clear-cut as Alex and Meagan's. There might be a benefit in making only part of your RRSP contribution to take you to a lower tax bracket, then using the refund to save for your big expense. A financial planner can help you find what will work.

If you're not saving to buy a home, go to school or start your own business, or if you don't expect any great leaps forward in your future income, the best thing you can do is maximize your RRSP contributions.

Spousal RRSPs

You can contribute all or part of your RRSP allowance to your spouse's RRSP and apply the tax benefit to your own income. This is especially useful when one person makes less than the other, or when one person will get a pension and the other won't. If you can't afford to pay the maximum into both RRSPs, make sure the person with the higher income is contributing the maximum in order to get the bigger tax advantage.

One thing to know about spousal RRSPs is that if you take the money out within three years of the last contribution, it will be added to the

$3,000 Extra a Year for Han and Fei

Han is a self-employed accountant earning about $75,000 a year. His wife, Fei, stays home with the kids. Every year he puts half of his contribution into his own RRSP and the other half into hers. He gets the full tax benefit for his contribution, even though it's not all going into his own RRSP.

When they retire they will have two equal retirement incomes rather than just his big income. As he draws income from his RRSP and she draws income from hers, they'll pay less tax than if they were drawing a larger amount from one RRSP. Instead of taking $75,000 from his RRSP for the year,, each of them can take $37,500 and be taxed at at a lower rate. They'll just have to decide what to do with the over $3,000 they're pocketing in tax savings.

$1,100 More in Edie and Sam's Pockets

Edie works at the gas company. When she retires, she'll receive a pension of $3,150 a month. Sam used to work at the gas company but he quit and used his retirement benefits to start his own consulting business. He'll get no pension beyond what he's saved in his RRSP. Edie and Sam both max out their RRSPs, but by the time they retire, his RRSP will provide him with only $2,200 a month. Meanwhile, at the rate she's saving, her RRSP will provide her with an extra $1,000 a month on top of her pension. She'll be taxed on $49,800 and he'll be taxed on $26,400. If she contributed to his RRSP so they'd be even when they retired, they would each be taxed on $38,100. Same retirement income, but the annual difference is over $1,100 more in their pockets.

taxable income of the person who contributed the money. And darned if that isn't the person who's in the higher tax bracket anyway!

BORROWING FOR YOUR RRSPS

It makes brilliant sense to borrow for your RRSP if you don't have the ready cash. Borrow an amount that you can afford to pay back monthly within a year. If you borrow $4,000 you'll be paying back an average of $333 per month plus interest. A couple of months after you file your income tax you'll get a refund of $1,600 (if you're in a 40% tax bracket) which you can use to pay back part of the loan. This will reduce your number of payments from 12 months to approximately seven months. Now you have a $4,000 RRSP earning money for you. Since you can afford to pay $333 every month, continue to make that contribution for this year's RRSP. Five months of saving $333 a month gives you $1,665 to contribute. Borrow $4,000 to add to it and this year you'll be able to contribute $5,665 to your RRSP. You'll then get a refund of $2,266. Pay that toward your RRSP loan and this time it will take you only five months to pay it back. And on it goes. After a few years you don't need to borrow the money anymore.

If these numbers make your eyes glaze over, just know that this a painless way of maxing out your RRSP—as long as you can afford to pay the loan back in one year. And it's especially useful for non-Savers because it's a forced saving plan. Another advantage is that you can put that money to work for you earlier in the year.

CONTRIBUTING EARLY

This is old news, but it never hurts to repeat good advice. Contribute to your RRSP as early in the year as possible, or contribute regularly throughout the year. Give your money more time to grow, and avoid the crazed rush at RRSP time.

There are two good reasons to avoid the RRSP-season madness. First, you won't be caught up in the frenzy so you'll be able to consider your investments more carefully. Second, and more important, dollar cost averaging provides better returns. Figure 8.2 illustrates the difference between contributing on March 1 and leaving your money in for an extra year instead of contributing on February 28, the last day for contributions.

Figure 8.2: Contribute Early, *i.e.*, on March 1 Instead of February 28

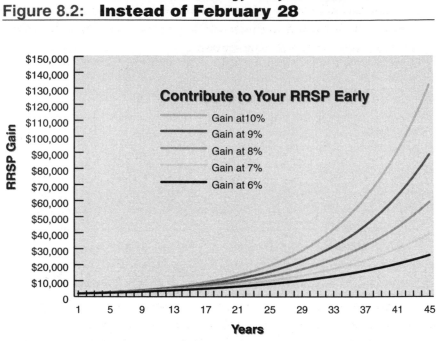

RRSPS AND KIDS

Some people think it's a great idea to start building up RRSPs for the kids. I don't. There's no tax advantage to you or to them, and there's even a chance that you're going to cost them money. But that doesn't mean you should completely ignore the idea of RRSPs and kids. There's always the carry-forward.

Say little Alana has a paper route and delivers flyers. She earns $1,500 per year. Make sure she files a tax return. She won't have to pay any tax on that money, but 18% of it, $270, is eligible for an RRSP contribution. Over five years, she'll build up $1,350 in tax-reducing RRSP contribution room. She can carry this forward until she needs it, possibly when she's CEO of the newspaper chain and earning $300,000 a year.

MAXIMIZING YOUR RRSPS

Here are the smartest ways to make your RRSPs work for you:
- Max 'em out every year (except in the rare cases I've mentioned).
- If you don't have the money to invest, borrow what you can afford to pay back in one year.

- Start young. The earlier in your life you start contributing, the more time your money has to compound and grow. $1,000 a year when you're in your twenties will do you more good than $2,000 a year when you're in your forties.
- Reinvest your tax refund. Plough it back into your RRSP.
- Don't wait till the last minute. Invest early and/or invest regularly so your money has longer to work for you.
- Take advantage of spousal RRSPs if you can.
- Consider consolidating your investments under one financial institution. You'll be able to follow them more easily.
- Designate your spouse as your beneficiary. This will defer tax and probate fees until your spouse's death. (More on this in Chapter 12.)
- Know how much is Enough, and how much you need to save to get there.

REGISTERED EDUCATION SAVINGS PLANS (RESPs)

The number one concern of most parents is to launch their children with the greatest possible array of opportunities. To this end, RESPs are absolutely wonderful for anyone with kids. Every year until your child is 17, you can put away up to $4,000 toward your child's post-secondary education and invest it any way you like. The government will match any portion of your first $2,000 with a 20% grant, the Canada Education Savings Grant (CESG). Over 17 years that can add up to $7,200 free from the government, plus what that money earns. I recommend just contributing the part that the government will match. If you have more to save, you can save it outside the RESP and your children can have access to it later with no strings attached.

MICAH TAKES ADVANTAGE OF GOVERNMENT RESP GRANT

Micah invested $2,000 after-tax dollars in a mutual fund as an RESP for his daughter. The government gave him a further $400 which he invested in the same mutual fund. The fund grew by 7% a year. The next year he did the same thing. At the end of two years, he had $5,341.44 on a total investment of $4,000. After 17 years of contributions from Micah and the government along with the compounded growth within the mutual fund, the RESP is worth $74,017—more than double his contributions, as you can see in Figure 8.3.

Figure 8.3: **The RESP Advantage**

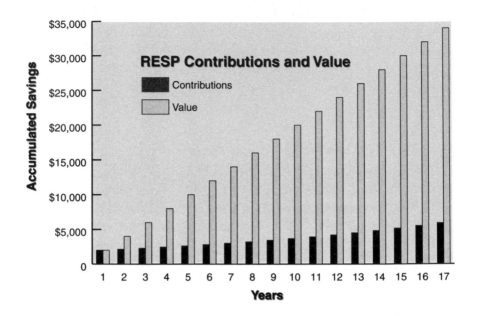

And that's not even the best part. All that money is tax-sheltered, meaning that you pay no taxes on the investment returns. RESPs have carry-forwards too, just like RRSPs, so if you can't contribute one year, you can make it up later. Within 25 years of the time you start the RESP, your child can use the money for tuition, supplies, accommodation or anything else to do with full-time post-secondary courses lasting 10 weeks or more. These include university, college, institutes of technology, apprenticeships or vocational school. Your kids will have to pay tax on the money, but for starving students, taxes are negligible.

Apart from finding the money to save, the only requirement is that you register each child for a Social Insurance Number. Be sure to put the RESP in both parents' names, because if you do end up putting the money in your RRSPs, the chances are there will be more contribution room available in two RRSPs than in one.

If child number one doesn't use the money, you can roll over your original contribution and the growth to the next child, but the government will take back its original grant money. If you don't have another child and the one you have (obviously switched at birth) is severely edu-phobic, the government will take back its grants—and again, not the growth on those grants—and you can contribute what's left to your RRSP, as long as you have RRSP contribution room. If your kids aren't considering going post-secondary, it might be helpful to remind them that you'll get it all if they don't use it. This might be just the nudge they need.

The absolute worst that can happen is that you'll have to pay tax on the growth. Is this a no-brainer, or what? Whether your kid becomes a rocket scientist or not, you still end up with something to be pretty pleased about.

Finding the Money for RESPs

The next question, of course, is "And just where do I get the money for my kids' education when I'm paying a mortgage, supporting a family, and supposedly putting money away for my own retirement as well?" I hear this question all the time, and it's definitely a tough one. Here are some possibilities.

START EARLY

When you start early, your money has more time to grow, so you can contribute less.

CONTRIBUTE WHAT YOU CAN

You might not be able to pay for your kids' entire post-secondary education, but you can help. Say $50 a month is all you can afford. That's still $600 per year, which qualifies for a grant of $120. After 17 years, at a 6% return, you'll have put away $21,532.07, all for about the cost of one family night at the movies per month.

CONTRIBUTE REGULARLY

As with any investment, if you spread your investment over the year rather than contributing a lump sum once a year, your money will have more time to grow, and dollar-cost averaging will even out the costs of your investments. It's easier on you as well—no last-minute scramble to find the money.

ASK THE GRANDPARENTS FOR HELP

Doting grandparents can be encouraged to contribute to their grandchildren's futures as well as their presents. In lieu of some gifts, suggest that grandparents contribute to the children's RESPs. Again, even a little will build up over time.

Not all your contributions to your kids' education will be financial. You can help them in other ways too.

ENCOURAGE THE KIDS TO LIVE AT HOME

Figure several thousand dollars a year extra for your students-to-be to live away from home. Of course, if they live at home, it will still cost you something, but you're already spending that money on them anyway. Even if they can go to a local college for two years, that's money you didn't need to save up. It's also a good deal for them: if they're going to school or working and saving for school, they live at home for free.

ENCOURAGE THE KIDS TO GET JOBS

If kids know from the start that they're going to have to contribute to their own education (and if they get a little shove in the direction of self-reliance from the parents), they'll accept the fact more readily. There's a certain independence that goes with having a job, and once they've tasted it, they'll get to like it.

HELP INVESTIGATE SCHOLARSHIPS AND BURSARIES

There's an ocean of scholarship and bursary money out there for all sorts of students with all sorts of interests from all sorts of backgrounds. Post-secondary institutions keep excellent listings of what's available, your municipal, provincial and federal government can help and your public library may also have up-to-date listings of grants, scholarships and bursaries.

SAVING OUTSIDE THE GOVERNMENT PLANS

If you can comfortably max out your RRSP and you still have money to invest, here's another place for it. Oh, I can hear the howls of protest now: "What? Save more? I've got kids, a mortgage, I'm maxing out my RRSP—what more do you want, lady??!!!" If you're taking care of all of that, congratulations. I agree, it's hard. You're doing a wonderful job. But if you can do more, you might as well. Here's why.

Non-RRSP savings are extremely useful for big-ticket items you buy before you retire (new car, vacation house etc.) and for extra income after you retire. You've already paid taxes on the original investment, so there's no tax to pay on the principal, unlike RRSP money. Whenever you draw money from your RRSP it is considered income and is therefore 100%

taxable, but with non-RRSP funds, only the growth is subject to tax. I recommend that you aim for equal amounts inside and outside your RRSP by the time you retire.

Before You Retire

There are two good reasons to save outside your RRSP for big-ticket items. First, you don't want to diminish the compounding power of your RRSP money by using those funds for big purchases. Let that money stay there accumulating and growing so you'll have regular income when you retire.

Second, if you dip into your RRSP before you retire, you *will* regret it. The heavy penalties for doing so are a ball and chain. That money will be added to your income for the year and you will be taxed at your highest marginal tax rate. So not only will you have to remove the cost of the purchase from your RRSP, you'll have to remove enough on top of that amount to pay your taxes owing. On what planet does that make sense?

CHRIS'S EXPENSIVE CAR

Chris makes $50,000 a year and wants to buy one of those cute VW Beetles. She takes $25,000 out of her RRSP because she wants to pay cash and avoid all the interest payments. A worthy sentiment indeed, except now her income is $75,000 for the year and that puts her in a higher tax bracket. Because she's so broke that she has to take money out of her RRSP for the car, she certainly doesn't have money lying around to pay the extra taxes, so that will have to come out of her RRSP too. Yow! By the time she takes out enough to cover the taxes and the car, she's borrowed over $36,000+ out of her RRSP.

Not only does Chris spend $36,000 to get the car, she loses all the compounding power of that $36,000 inside her RRSP. She might as well have borrowed $100,000 from the bank and bought a Jaguar convertible!

If there's a big-ticket item on your horizon, save for it outside your RRSP. You can put your RRSP refund toward it, or you can put a portion of your savings in your RRSP and save the rest outside it for a few years. You'll be able to catch up later with your carry-forwards.

You don't have a crystal ball, so often you don't foresee major expenses coming up. At the very least, try to build yourself a cushion of three months' salary in case of emergency.

AFTER YOU RETIRE

Once you retire, savings and investments outside your RRSP can augment your income without adding to your tax burden. Your RRSP retirement income will be taxed at the same rate as your income now. Income from non-RRSP savings won't be. The original savings were after-tax money. Only their growth will be taxed.

Another thing to remember is that different kinds of investment returns are taxed at different rates. Interest from bonds, GICs, T-bills and savings accounts is 100% taxable, but income from dividends, and capital gains yielded by stocks, mutual funds, real estate, commodities and other investments are taxed at a lower rate.

Guaranteed investments that pay interest should always be inside your RRSP. Eventually you'll have to pay 100% tax on the money, but until you start taking income, the interest is tax sheltered. Outside your RRSP you have to pay the tax on all of your interest every year, because you get a T-5 slip that you must declare. Your owner-type investments should be outside your RRSP where they are treated as capital gains. The growth on these investments is 50% tax free. But if they're in your RRSP, once you

---

COVERING TONY AND JULIA'S TRAVEL PLANS FOR RETIREMENT

Tony and Julia figure they'll be more than comfortable living on $74,000 a year after they retire. This will allow them to receive $37,000 each and remain in the lowest tax bracket. Early in their retirement they want to do a lot of travelling and they figure that will cost about $15,000 a year extra. If they've saved outside their RRSPs, the extra $15,000 is available without adding to their taxable income. If they haven't, it's going to cost them. They'll have to take an extra $24,000 to cover the travel and the taxes on the extra income. And it could get worse if they suddenly need a new roof and have to deplete their RRSPs even more. Not only that, they're knocking the heck out of the compounding power of their RRSPs.

start taking an income, it's 100% taxable, regardless of what the original investment was. You also have control over when you sell these investments, which makes tax planning easier.

Even if you're a dedicated Spender, Giver or Builder, don't the twin miracles of compounding returns and tax breaks make you want to save a couple of hundred dollars a month at least? RRSPs and RESPs are two extraordinary gifts from the government. They force you to save if you have trouble saving, they reward you almost immediately for your efforts and they punish you if you withdraw too soon. On top of that, they are shells that protect your compounding investments from being eaten up by taxes as you go through the ages and stages of your life— and those are what I'll look at in the next chapter.

CHAPTER

AGES AND STAGES

One of the greatest labour-saving devices of today is tomorrow. — Vincent T. Foss

Much of what you *should* be doing depends on your age and stage in life. Somebody who's young and unencumbered has time to make mistakes and take big risks. Someone who's middle-aged, paying a mortgage and looking at putting kids through university needs to protect that principal and make it grow at the same time. Here are the basic strategies for each age and stage.

AGE 20 - 35

It's hard at this age to think about the fact that someday you really will get old and retire—so don't. Build toward your dreams and goals instead. The first thing to invest in at this stage is yourself. This is when you go to school, upgrade your skills in your field, make contacts, start a business.

Have a Plan

Even if your first priority right now is to have fun, somewhere along the line there will be things you want to achieve, things you want to have. Do you know what you want? The wish list and Yearly Goals in Chapter 3 are great exercises to help you clarify your desires. They're especially useful if you're not particularly focused or ambitious.

Don't Borrow Too Much

If you're going to school, think hard about how much you really need in student loans. Any money you borrow now will have to be paid back with after-tax dollars once you graduate, and there is absolutely no fun in starting your working life with a $40,000 debt hanging over your head. The worst case I ever saw was a young woman who graduated as a doctor with $60,000 in student debt. Her payments started at $900 a month. If this had been the only way she could become a doctor, it might have been understandable, but she had spent every summer of her university career vacationing in Europe.

Can you work all summer instead of taking that one course you want? Is there any part-time work you can do during the school year that doesn't interfere too much with your studies (and doesn't completely wipe out your social life)? Can you stretch out your education by one more year so you can work part-time more easily? Do you qualify for any bursaries or scholarships? Can you go to school and live at home at the same time, even just for the first couple of years? Anything you can do now will mean a better start and a more carefree future.

Start a Saving Habit

Your twenties are the best time to get started saving at least 10% off the top and putting it away. You're used to not having a lot of money, especially if you've just come off being a starving student. Now that you've finally got an income, you won't even notice the money off the top. This is money that will be invested or be spent on things that increase in value: a home, further education, equipment for your home business etc. As soon as you can afford to, get started on your RRSPs as well. It's tempting to think that you might as well wait until you're in your high-earning years and you'll make up the difference by doubling up your contributions. But look at the difference between $1,000 invested from age 25 on and $2,000 invested from age 45-on. The same amount of money is contributed, with a big difference in the results. (See Figure 9.1). You should definitely be contributing by age 30. Chapter 8, on RRSPs, can give you the details about when to save inside or outside an RRSP.

If you *are* saddled with student debt (or any other kind, for that matter), use the 10% or more to pay off your loan as quickly as possible, because paying off debt *is* saving. The faster you get it done, the less interest you'll pay and the quicker you can start to enjoy your money.

Use Your Youthful Energy

At your age you can work all day, party all night and still be ready to bite a tiger the next day. Oddly enough, this phase of your life does not last—

Figure 9.1:   **Start Your RRSP Early**

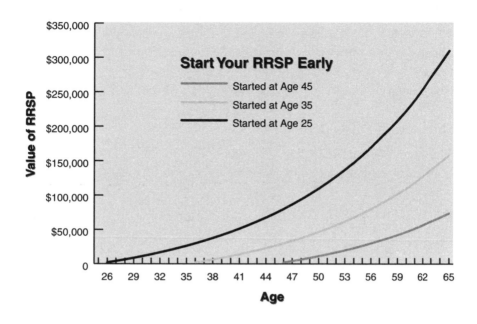

ask anybody who's over 40. So take advantage of it. If you have a dream, now's the time to invest your energy in reaching it, whether you're working 80-hour weeks at a small software company you own share options in, taking on extra freelance jobs to save for a two-year trip around the world or staying up every night to write your opera.

This is also when you can take on an extra job or extra work to get yourself out of debt as quickly as possible—short-term pain for long-term gain. When you're young, work is often a big part of your social life anyway, so it doesn't seem quite so arduous.

If you're not willing to give up so much of your free time, at least consider taking a few classes (tax deductible) that will help you build your career—or find out what you want your career to be.

Take Some Risks

Young people know and understand what's new. You can feel the currents. This is your huge advantage over older people. Young people were the ones who saw the potential of the Internet long before anyone else. You're the ones who can't imagine life without cell phones. You're the first to live in a cheap neighbourhood that's on its way up. The popular culture and new technology you understand so well offer wonderful opportunities to start your own business or get in on the ground floor of some investments. Ask yourself, if I like this, need this, use this, want this, will others? What's considered cool in my field/age group/region? Why?

At your age, you can build an aggressive investment portfolio or start a business on a shoestring (not neglecting prudent business practices, of course). You might lose, but you have time in your life to recover. On the other hand, if you win . . .well, as people my age used to say, far out.

Start a Good Credit History

There will come a time when you need to borrow money—for a house, a business or something else that's important to you. If you start using credit responsibly now, you'll get that money when you need it. From the moment you get your first phone bill, you are building a credit history. If you pay your bills on time you'll be seen as more reliable (well, duh!) and this will one day matter. So once you're on the radar, fly right. Pay your bills by their due date. I've heard of people who used to let their phone and electricity bills ride for a few months before paying them and then were surprised when they were turned down for credit. "But I always pay them eventually" isn't good enough.

Restrict yourself to one credit card (another one for the business, if you have a business) and get in the habit of paying it in full every month, or over the course of a few months if you've bought something big. Having credit cards doesn't necessarily mean you have a good credit rating. Credit card companies are a lot looser about lending you money than banks. Usually they're charging you a higher interest rate, so the more you owe the better for them, as long as you're paying the minimum payment. Banks, on the other hand, are very conservative by nature and leave no room for error. If you have a bad credit rating and want to borrow from a bank, you might not get anything at all, or you might have to pay significantly higher interest than your neighbour who has a good credit rating.

Try to Get on the Same Page Financially

If there are two of you, you might as well start off right. Few things can sour a relationship like money battles. Somehow that guy you married isn't as sexy or funny when you realize his credit rating's in the tank and you can't get a mortgage. That vision of loveliness who shares your bed doesn't have quite the same appeal when she insists on keeping all her money to herself.

Different attitudes, different aspirations—these can drive a wedge between two people. But if you agree on how to handle money and what to spend it on, other problems become quite small. If you haven't done so already, both of you should do The Attitude Quiz starting on page 11 (Figure 1.1). Knowing each other's attitudes is a big part of understanding each other's behaviour. You can plan your finances in a way that gives both of you some leeway to express yourselves.

No doubt when you were getting to know each other you talked a lot about your goals and dreams. Now here's a chance to do it again. The wish list and Yearly Goals in Chapter 3 are even more important when there are two of you. Make your wish lists separately, then compare them to see which ones you can work on first. You can compare your Yearly Goals as well, if you wish. It's pretty important to know if one of you wants to go back to school and the other wants to start a family. You'll have to make some priorities. On page 36 you'll find some advice about how the two of you can achieve different Wish List goals without coming to blows.

Do your estate planning. You may be young, but that doesn't mean you're invincible. You have to think about each other's futures now. Look at Chapter 12 for a rundown on what you have to consider.

Finally, how do you both feel about risk? That's something else to consider. If one of you is financially fearless and the other's only interested in interest, you may have to set some ground rules, or get a financial planner who can carve out a middle road that suits you both.

If You Want Kids, Build Some Reserves

Kids cost—somewhere over $200,000 per child if you include a higher education. So what are you doing to prepare? If both of you work once you have children, you won't have the same disposable income you enjoy now because you'll have to pay for daycare or a nanny. And if one of you stays home, which is a choice I see a lot of young people making, you'll definitely feel the pinch. You're used to two incomes. It's going to be very difficult to cut back to one, never mind the fact that you'll have extra mouths to feed.

One of the best things you can do in preparation is live on one income before you start your family. Use the other income to get ahead of the game: save for a house or pay down big chunks of your mortgage, build up a fund for later and/or take care of your RRSPs. A few years of that and you'll be in excellent shape when you do have a family, even if you both plan to work. Your mortgage payments will be more manageable and you'll have some money put away for when you need it. Breathing room.

The choice between both parents working and one staying home is a very personal one. A number of my clients have had one parent stay home and they have truly enjoyed it. They say that they can't have all the things their friends have, but what they give up in material things they make up in time together as a family. It's not easy these days, but it can be done.

If You Have Kids, Plan Ahead

Understanding each other's attitudes to money and risk and making plans for your family's future are absolutely vital. You may not be able to start investing or saving just yet, but the time will come. And you will have to agree on where to draw the line on spending for your kids. Some people who would never dream of spending $100 on something for themselves will blow it happily on something their kids don't really need or want, but that was so-o-o-o cute they couldn't resist. If you have widely diverging attitudes, it might be an idea to invoke the 48-hour rule (page 72).

You'll also want to think about your children's future. Even a few hundred dollars a year in an RESP will lessen your burden when they move on to higher education. And if you have a child with disabilities that will make independent living difficult, you definitely want to start putting something away. If your parents are eager to give the kids gifts, maybe you could suggest that the best gift of all would be money in an RESP or trust. That might give you a bit of budget leeway to contribute to your own RRSPs, pay down the mortgage faster or to spend more time with your kids instead of working overtime.

Remember that living within your means is not a sin. Your kids may have to learn that they won't automatically get everything they want. It won't do them any harm.

Single Parents, Set a Path

The best money managers I've ever seen have been single parents— because they have no choice. The single person with kids faces the greatest challenge, financially and emotionally. If this is your situation, just know it's difficult, but not impossible.

One of your biggest dilemmas is balancing your desire to get yourself and your family ahead against your desire to spend time with your family (and, on those rare occasions, by yourself). At this age, even though you have kids, you should put as much as you can into building your skills so you can get a well-paid job. Your parents might be able to babysit while you go to school or work, and you may be able to take advantage of government programs that will help finance your education.

If you're looking for a job, find out what each company offers in terms of medical, dental and life insurance coverage and how the pension plan works. If you can find a job with better benefits, it might be worth taking a small reduction in salary in exchange.

If you're already working, you might not be able to save for your retirement just yet, but do try to put away a little bit here and there to build an emergency fund. With no partner to take up the slack, you need an emergency fund more than anyone. Difficult as it is, you need to avoid letting all your money slip away and having to live from cheque to cheque. The 10% rule comes in handy here, but if you just can't survive with 10% taken off your gross earnings, at least try for 5%. Taking it off the top—at the source if possible—eases the temptation to spend every cent you make. As to the temptation to borrow, well, you know my general philosophy on that if you've read this far. In the case of a single parent, especially one who's close to the line anyway, getting into debt can be like stepping into quicksand: it's much more difficult for you to get out. Borrow only if the payments are well within your budget.

Dealing with an ex can be horrible, especially if one person has appreciably more money than the other. On top of the pain the breakup has caused, the kids are bounced between two different standards of living. ("Well if I can't get it from you I'll just get it from Dad.") If it's at all possible to communicate, make a pact with your ex about how money will be spent on the kids. A mediator experienced in working with families can help anticipate problems and find equitable solutions—and having a third party involved decreases some of the tensions that can make people react irrationally.

Sometimes a pact is out of the question. If so, don't get caught up in competing with the other parent. That way lies madness. Let your kids know what they can expect from you and what you expect from them. Do what you can. It's all you can do.

Finally, don't feel guilty. You can waste a lot of time and energy—money too—trying to compensate for being a single parent. Give yourself a break and don't compare yourself with other families or with some impossible ideal. Settle on your own values and stick with them. You'll have to be creative about ways to have fun without spending money and you'll have to watch the food and clothing budget carefully, but kids won't feel hard-done-by over those things until they're older (and when they're older, *all* kids feel hard-done-by, not just yours). In the meantime, what they really need is the knowledge that they are loved. You can give them that for free.

AGE 35 - 50

(Note that I didn't call this middle age.) By now you're probably settled in your career and your home and have some savings put away. Your parents might be feeling the effects of age or illness, so it's starting to dawn on you that this will someday come to you as well. The closer you get to retirement, the less fuzzy it looks, and you're beginning to get serious about making sure you have a good one. So . . .

Pay Down the Mortgage

If you're single, a couple without kids or a couple whose kids are grown, double up and get your mortgage paid off. If you max out your RRSPs every year, you can apply the refund to your mortgage to bring it down early. Once you've paid for the house you'll have a lot more disposable income. Enjoy some of it and start building a portfolio outside your RRSPs to give you extra, non-taxable income when you retire.

Max Out Your RRSPs

I know, I know. At this age you have so many responsibilities that it's really hard to save. But you're coming into your peak earning years. First of all, you want to make the most of those RRSP tax breaks. Second, you've got more money than you had before. If you take 18% off the top for your RRSPs, are you really going to notice it? (You sure will when you're retired and you've got a nice cushy income to live on.)

Start Some Non-Registered Savings

Oooh, this one gets nasty reactions. But even before retirement it's handy to have a fund that will take care of home and car repairs, big trips and other big and sometimes unexpected expenses.

Plan for the Worst

Consult your financial planner about making or updating your will, and get insured if you have family who depend on you. You might also want to investigate critical illness insurance, which can provide a lump sum of money that helps families through the expensive ordeal of a serious illness and might even enable them to do some things they've always wanted to do together. There's more on insurance at the end of this chapter.

Protect Your Principal

At this age you want to become a bit more conservative in your investments. You don't have to eliminate all risk, but you need to make sure that you're not going to lose most of what you've so painstakingly built up over the years. By all means, stay in the stock market as a long-term investor, and own a couple of aggressive mutual funds, but try to speculate only with money that's profit from something else. Don't buy and sell like a day trader—you'll eat up too much of your earnings in brokerage fees. Remember, it's time in the market, not market timing, that makes the difference. If you love risk, you're pretty safe devoting 10% of your portfolio to risky investments.

Reward Yourself

Check out your wish list from Chapter 3 and see what you can afford. You've earned it!

AGE 50 - 65

First, make sure you'll have Enough. The closer you are to retirement, the more realistic your Enough projections will be. For the five years before you retire, run your numbers once a year, and take another look at your Yearly Goals and wish list. Can you accomplish what you want with the money you have?

Clear Up Debt

If you have any debt, clear it up—because it will be much harder to clear it up when you're living off your savings and investments. Nothing worries imminent retirees like debt. If you have the slightest twinge of doubt about your situation, seek out a second opinion. I've observed that most people have a reliable gut reaction when they're receiving financial advice that is somehow out of whack.

A Late Start but Sylvie Pulls it Off

Sylvie had gone through her married life as a socialite, but at 55 she and her husband divorced. His business had faltered in the few years leading up to the divorce, so when the assets were divided, she didn't get much. She had just enough to buy a condominium with a little left over to invest. It was a situation that could knock the will out of many people, but Sylvie was marvellous. For the first time since she married, she went to work. She simplified her life and started saving whatever she could and investing carefully.

Sylvie worked until she was 67, then decided she had enough. Her retirement savings only amounted to something under $200,000, but along with Old Age Security and half of her ex-husband's CPP, it provides her with an income of $2,000 a month. She is able to visit her daughter in the east once in a while and has also been to visit relatives in Europe. Part of her secret is that she draws pleasure from simple things. If she has a glass of wine or a delicious dinner, she savours it. A sunset gives her joy. But the other part is that she knew what she had to do and did it.

Are You Doing Anything After Work?

Retirement can seem like an end in itself, but really it's just a beginning. Unless you want to spend the rest of your life watching Regis Philbin, better get interested in something beyond work. Chapter 11 talks about how to prepare yourself.

Better Late than Never

If you're just starting to save for retirement now, don't lose hope. You can still give yourself a modest monthly income. You'll have to save all you can now, and possibly work longer than you intended to, but it can be done. You might want to try living on your projected retirement income early so you can add more savings to the pot. At the very least you'll get used to what you're going to be living on, and if you're able to top up your savings enough, you may even be giving yourself a long-term raise. If there are two of you working, live on one income and sock the rest away in RRSPs and non-registered savings. You won't believe how fast your resources will grow.

By 55 most of your debt is gone (I hope). Max out your RRSPs and use up any carry-forward room. Save as well in non-registered funds for retirement and for larger purchases. Even if you can only build up $250,000, at a modest 6% return you'll get an income of $15,000 a year without counting Canada Pension Plan and Old Age Security.

You may not be able to retire completely as soon as you'd like. You may have to take a part-time job for a while to make ends meet, and the longer you can put off dipping into your retirement savings, the more time they have to build up. But you *can* do it. Money makes money. It will work for you too. Chapter 11 will offer you a few more hints on enjoying your retirement years – and ensuring that your savings last as long as you do.

INSURANCE

At every age and every stage, insurance can be important. I've seen various kinds of insurance make a huge difference in people's lives. It's not something you do for yourself. You do it because you love somebody. Givers, this should really appeal to you. Builders like it too because it protects their businesses. But how on earth do you know what insurance is right for you?

Life Insurance

Life insurance is when you're betting you'll die and you're hoping that you'll lose the bet. Consider it a necessary evil, but the reality is that people do die, or become disabled or ill, and if they've bought the right amount of life insurance, their families don't have to go begging. Not only do the beneficiaries receive the money in the policy, they receive it tax free.

One of my uncles wanted to make sure his family would be taken care of if something happened to him, but he bought far more insurance than he needed. I saw him struggling throughout his working life to pay for it. If I'd known then what I know now, I would have told him my simple rule of thumb: replace your income. Although insurance is paid in a lump sum, think of it as income and plan it accordingly. For example, a $1 million life insurance policy invested at a 7% annual return would replace an income of $70,000 a year. Replacing income isn't the only concern. If one of you doesn't work outside the home, what would it cost to pay for a nanny or household help to replace the contributions of the person who stayed home?

There are three types of life insurance: Term, Universal and Whole Life. Insurance is very complicated. The industry uses terms you've never heard in your life, and each company can give the same type of policy a completely different name. I won't bore you with details. Your insurance representative or financial advisor can fill you in. But here are the basics.

TERM INSURANCE

If you have any non-deductible debt (car loan, mortgage, credit card, any other personal loan), then just buy term insurance. Term is the cheapest, and the money you would save by not buying more expensive insurance can be used to pay down your debt. When you can afford it, you can get the more expensive types. Term insurance is inexpensive when you're young, then escalates a lot as you get older, although at any point it can usually be converted into some form of permanent insurance, which has more stable premiums. There's also the disadvantage that you won't get back what you put into it. But as a stopgap measure for people with young families, it's a good deal.

WHOLE LIFE INSURANCE

Whole life covers your whole life, just as it says. The premiums are usually fixed and you may or may not keep paying for it your whole life. At some time in your life you can elect premium offset, which means no more premiums are required. Many whole life policies are called Participating Life because you're participating in the profits of the company. These policies have a guaranteed cash value as well as dividends paid from the profits of the company.

You may borrow up to 90% of the total cash value of the policy. Many people have found that their life insurance policies have saved them in difficult times, personally or in their businesses. Though they hadn't realized it at the time, a whole life policy turned out to be a forced savings plan. Sometimes people have used the cash value on retirement to supplement their income, because the cash value of a whole life policy can be converted to an annuity, and there can be some tax advantages to doing this.

UNIVERSAL LIFE INSURANCE

The difference between universal life and whole life is that with whole life you're leaving the investing of the proceeds in your policy to the insurance company.

In the universal product, after you've paid the expenses, taxes and insurance fees, you can invest the balance of your accumulated premiums in various options that the insurance company provides through term deposits or index funds. It's much more active management on your part, and you can make the decisions on your own or with the help of your insurance advisor. The proceeds in the policy will only do as well as the markets are doing.

There are two big advantages to universal life. First, any growth within the policy is tax-deferred. Second, you can prepay your premiums. If you pay them off during your top earning years, you can retire without having any life insurance payments to make.

There are two other types of insurance that can make important contributions to your peace of mind.

DISABILITY INSURANCE

Disability insurance replaces your income during your working years when you are unable to work as a result of either permanent or temporary disabilities. The government only allows you to collect $66\frac{2}{3}\%$ of your income from insurance tax-free. Long-term disability coverage at work may completely cover your former income. If not, if you have a high income, you may need to buy additional private disability insurance to take you to that level. When you're self-employed, this is the most important insurance you can have. Any kind of disability that makes it impossible for you to work will eat up your savings very quickly and even put you in debt. If you're in business for yourself, get it. Period. If your budget is limited, at least put something in place so you have some protection.

There are different waiting periods before you can collect. The longer you wait, once disabled, the lower the price of the policy. If you want to wait only 30 days before you start collecting, you'll pay more than someone willing to wait for 90 days. Another decision you have to make is how long you will be able to collect the benefits after you become disabled. You can be covered for two years, five years or until you're 65. The shorter the waiting period and the longer the benefit period, the more you'll pay.

You can also buy riders that cover lifetime accident insurance, cost of living, partial disability, or guaranteed purchase options (where once you own a policy you can increase your coverage even if you're no longer insurable).

CRITICAL ILLNESS

This type of insurance is fairly new. It covers certain illnesses like cancer or heart disease. If you've been diagnosed, you get a large lump sum which you can use in whatever way you want. Often in the U.S. the benefit is used to defray medical costs. It hasn't been as popular in Canada because of our greater access to the medical system. But for people who have been diagnosed with something life threatening and who want to do something with their families or live out a dream, it's a good thing.

EMPLOYEE BENEFITS

Before you buy insurance, find out what you're already covered for at work— yes, I'm talking about actually reading the booklet they gave you. Before you need to. If you don't understand it, go to someone in Human Resources or check with your financial advisor.

I'll provide more information about the tax and estate implications of life insurance in Chapter 12, but I do want to pass on a vote of confidence in life insurance companies. My own experience with insurance companies is that they not only do what they're contracted to do, they do it within the spirit of the contract.

One of my clients worked on a fishing boat that went down in a terrible storm. No trace of it was found. The insurance company didn't have to pay for seven years because there was no body found, but rather than see the family go through any hardship, they paid in six months because they knew there was no doubt about what had happened.

Another man I knew was diagnosed with cancer and went down to Florida to spend his remaining days. He died there within six months, but he'd left home without paying his last life insurance premium. Although I hadn't sold him the policy, the family came to me for help, so I went to the company and told them that this man knew he was dying and had another insurance policy with me. He had paid that one up, and I knew he would not have deliberately let his other policy lapse. He had always paid all of his premiums on time, but with this one he had simply forgotten to provide the company with his new address so the notice didn't get to him. It is the insured's responsibility to make sure the premiums are paid and the insurance company was under no legal obligation to pay out, but they did, obeying the spirit of the contract, rather than the letter. I've developed a lot of respect for insurance companies in my years of working for and with them.

I combined ages and stages and life insurance in one chapter for a reason. When you're young, you never feel you're going to get ill or die. The younger you are, the more difficult it is to buy into the concept of life insurance. As you move through the ages and stages of your life, it becomes more apparent why you need to. Givers get it from the start. They're taking care of the ones they love and passing on a legacy. Spenders are inclined to be okay with the disability side but also say "Who cares, if I'm dead? I'd rather spend it myself than have someone else benefit!" Savers, once they really know they have enough for themselves, say "Okay, why not?" Builders are so busy building that they need someone to stop them and point out the merits of protecting what they've built.

Meanwhile, you're still here, and you may have noticed that throughout this book the phrase "if you own your own business" keeps reappearing. It's an option that more and more people are exercising, and in the next chapter I'll pass on the financial wisdom I've gained after years of dealing with people who've started and run their own companies—and my own experience too.

CHAPTER  10

THE ENTREPRENEURIAL OPTION

> *If anybody had ever told me how much work it would be,*
> *I would never have started this business.—Everyone who*
> *ever started a business (including me)*

It might have hit you like a bomb one morning when you realized that you just could not stand to walk into that same building every weekday anymore. Maybe it was an idea that got under your skin and niggled at you until you had to do something about it. Perhaps one day you realized that you could do this better than the people who were already doing it. It could have been a little sideline that you did for fun and people couldn't get enough. Or, at the age of 52, you were declared redundant.

In the last decade, more new businesses have started than ever before. Younger people see themselves as free agents, encouraged by true stories of businesses that started in somebody's parents' basement or garage and grew into multi-million dollar enterprises. Older types have felt the pinch of downsizing or grown weary of office politics. And, armed with no more than a computer, cell phone and fax machine, hundreds of thousands of people have decided to march to their own drummer.

Every business owner is prodded by a different impulse, but all of them will eventually face the same challenges. In my work as a financial planner I have been privy to the stories of hundreds of entrepreneurs, some successful, some not, and a few who go from success to failure and back as often as other people change their shoes. I've also run my own small business for the last 25 years, and much of what I put into practice I've learned from my clients. In this chapter I'll pass on some of the insights I've garnered from my position at ringside.

ARE YOU AN ENTREPRENEUR?

Nothing is more exciting and inspirational than starting your own business. You're learning something new all the time, and handling challenge after challenge. It's a combination of a little fear and a lot of excitement— and with that fear and excitement comes a lot of hard work.

Builder, Saver, Giver or Spender—it's not your financial attitude that determines if you can start and run a successful business, it's some other personality traits entirely. Nobody's going to ask you if you completed that project or got the cheques for employees out or wrote your business plan. Can you work on your own and keep yourself focused and motivated? Before you become your own boss, ask if you're the right person for the job. Figure 10.1 is a quiz you can take that will give you an idea. For each question, choose the sentence that best describes you and your attitude toward running your own business. Be honest. When you've finished, add up the numbers of each letter and see whether As, Bs, Cs or Ds predominate.

Figure 10.1: **Are You an Entrepreneur?**

1.   ❑ A Once I know something's required, I'll run with it.
     ❑ B Once I've established what is required, I can run with it.
     ❑ C Once I'm sure I know exactly what is required, I can make sure it's done properly.
     ❑ D Once somebody's told me what to do, I'll do it.

2.   ❑ A When things are running smoothly, I get bored.
     ❑ B When things are running smoothly, I analyze why and anticipate what could go wrong.
     ❑ C When things are running smoothly, I worry that it won't last.
     ❑ D When things are running smoothly, I relax.

3.   ❑ A I set my own deadlines and keep to them.
     ❑ B I use deadlines to help me set timelines.
     ❑ C I always try to have things finished well before a deadline.
     ❑ D I need deadlines to motivate me.

4.   ❑ A I get more ideas than I know what to do with.
     ❑ B I like to throw ideas around with other people.
     ❑ C I build ideas out of the information I receive.
     ❑ D I get a lot of ideas from reading and the media.

5. ❑ A When I'm working on a problem, I can forget to eat or sleep.
   ❑ B When I'm working on a problem, I make sure I eat and sleep.
   ❑ C When I'm working on a problem, I have trouble eating and sleeping.
   ❑ D When I'm working on a problem, I stop when it's time to eat or sleep.

6. ❑ A I tell people what to do and they can figure out the details themselves.
   ❑ B I tell people what to do and how to do it and try to motivate them to want to do it.
   ❑ C I tell people what to do and how to do it and then check on their progress often.
   ❑ D I ask people if it's okay with them to do what I want them to do.

7. ❑ A Waiting makes me crazy.
   ❑ B If I have to wait for something, I'll do something else in the meantime.
   ❑ C If I'm waiting for something, I always have something else that requires my attention.
   ❑ D If I have to wait for something, I consider that a well-earned break.

8. ❑ A If I need funds to take it to the next level, I'll get them.
   ❑ B If I need funds to take it to the next level, I'll make sure I'm not putting this level in jeopardy.
   ❑ C If I need funds to take it to the next level, I wonder if I've failed somehow.
   ❑ D Why should I take it to the next level? Everything's going fine the way it is.

9. ❑ A Fun is work.
   ❑ B For fun I like to refresh my mind by getting away from work.
   ❑ C Even when I have fun, part of me is still at work.
   ❑ D Work is no fun.

10. ❑ A When I envision something, I see the whole thing and then figure out the parts.
    ❑ B When I envision something, I imagine what goes into building it.
    ❑ C When I envision something, I keep getting tripped up by the difficult details.
    ❑ D When I envision something, I enjoy the fantasy.

11. ❑ A If I try something and it doesn't work out, at least I did everything I could to make it work.
    ❑ B If I try something and it doesn't work out, at least I've learned something.
    ❑ C If I try something and it doesn't work out, I tend to obsess over where I might have gone wrong.
    ❑ D If I try something and it doesn't work out, I probably should have worked harder at it.

12. ❏ A I trust my gut.
     ❏ B I try to back up my decisions with good research, but sometimes I have to trust my gut.
     ❏ C I can amass so much research that I have trouble making a decision.
     ❏ D I'd rather somebody else made the decisions.

13. ❏ A I don't need other people except to do what I tell them.
     ❏ B I value the ideas of other well-informed people.
     ❏ C I don't trust other people to do things the right way.
     ❏ D I like the social aspects of work.

14. ❏ A The riskier something is, the more interested I get.
     ❏ B The riskier something is, the more work needs to go into it to lessen the risk.
     ❏ C The riskier something is, the less I like it.
     ❏ D I played the slots in Las Vegas once.

15. ❏ A If I can't convince somebody I'm right, I'll keep at them until I do.
     ❏ B If I can't convince somebody I'm right, I'll see if I can make an end-run around them.
     ❏ C If I can't convince somebody I'm right, they're incapable of getting it anyway.
     ❏ D If I can't convince somebody I'm right, big deal.

A   Risk-Taker

The more your A answers outpace the others, the more risk-taking genes you were born with. You're the classic entrepreneurial type. You're creative—ahead of the pack in your thinking—and you attack anything you're interested in with a passion that sometimes blots out everything else. You've always felt self-sufficient, and could even be called a bit of a loner. You're determined, persistent, resourceful and hardworking. You often have several projects on the go at one time. The Risk-taker and the Builder are pretty much the same person.

And now for the bad news. You can lose interest in things just as fast as you fall in love with them, and when you let your attention lapse, things can get away from you. They might even get to the point where you're jumping from crisis to crisis instead of progressing. You're also not much for the myriad details that have to be dealt with in a business. You'd rather be making deals or serving customers in the store than cranking out invoices. This is another trait that can get you into frequent hot water—but then again, you crave the excitement.

You also tend to neglect yourself and those who love you (if anyone does). When you get into a serious relationship, your sweetie needs to know that you won't be around much because you consider work the most fun a human being can have. If your sweetie bolts, accept it. The right person is someone who understands the forces that drive you and is self-sufficient enough to live without your constant attention. The right person is also someone who can tell when you're driving yourself to exhaustion and has enough clout to make you slow down.

In business you need help, believe it or not. You need someone to follow you around and take care of the day-to-day running of the company as you concentrate on the big picture or your newest interest. You need someone you can trust when there's a difference of opinion. It has to be someone who can stand up to you when the situation calls for it, because you tend to want to mow down all dissenters. Get yourself a B to run your business(es) and maybe get yourself a C as your personal assistant.

B   Manager

You are the ideal person to run a business. You should have no trouble starting a business either, as long as you find a great idea to base it on. Unlike the Risk-taker, you're not easily distracted, and you know the importance of getting the boring day-to-day stuff under control. It may not make you dizzy with joy, but if it's done regularly and with good systems in place, the major crises can be avoided. Because you don't depend as much on excitement for your motivation, you're better than the Risk-taker at staying true to your course, even when not much is happening.

Whereas the Risk-taker relies on instinct a lot, you lead with your head. You learn from experience, you listen to others, you do the research. The best Managers listen to their instincts too, but not exclusively.

You understand the value of balance, in business and in your personal life. In business, you're not likely to put everything you have at risk so you can take a big leap into something else. In your personal life, you make time to be with your friends and loved ones, and you do your best to fit in rest and exercise.

If there's a downside, it may be that you lack that bit of fire, that aggression that gives you the ability to ambush venture capitalists as they leave their office. The Risk-taker does this kind of thing from passion. You may have to dig inside yourself a little to find the passion and let it guide you.

There's probably nobody better to start and run a business than a B who shows a lot of A attributes as well.

C   Detail Person

Engineers, accountants, scientists, programmers, librarians, researchers, editors, detectives, mechanics—all these people exhibit a flair for detail, and without them, where would the world be? This flair can be a good thing or a bad thing, depending on the type of business and on the person's other traits.

If you're a C, you are patient, methodical and curious. You like to know exactly how things work, and when you find something that does work, you will clutch it to your heart. On the other hand, if something doesn't work, you'll find a way to fix it, even if it takes forever. The challenge for you is finding the answers. Your curiosity is a boon when it comes to gathering or analyzing data, because you won't overlook a thing.

If your test results were straight Cs, you probably should be thinking about becoming a partner in a business rather than starting one of your own. It's too easy for you to get absorbed in the fine points and lose the vision. There's also the danger that you might run yourself ragged trying to take care of every little thing. You have a tendency to try to do everything yourself because, after all, nobody does it quite as well as you. Hook up with an A or B, and let them deal with the big things while you concentrate on splicing genes or correcting dangling gerunds.

If you're a C with a lot of A, now we're talkin'. You've got the creativity, drive and vision as well as the attention to little things that can make or break a business. I suspect a lot of software billionaires are C types with a good deal of A in the mix.

There's nothing wrong with a C and B mix, either. If you get a good idea—and let's face it, Risk-takers haven't cornered the market on those—you'll probably do a great job of researching the market and setting up your business properly before you open the doors. You might need help from a pit-bull sales force or capital raiser, but if you can discipline yourself to delegate and make yourself stop researching and *do* something, you'll probably do well.

D   Blithe Spirit

If most of your answers were D, especially 1, 4, 9, 12 and 13, you like security and don't care for too much responsibility. You value fun and relaxation too much to put in the hours to make a business work. Being in business for yourself would probably make you miserable. If you're unhappy in your job now, though, maybe what you need is a change. Go to the end of the chapter for some words about changing careers.

If I didn't know the working habits of some creative people, I would say that a D should never go into business. Yet I hear from some writers, graphic artists and others who freelance that what other people would call appalling work habits are the norm. These people develop creative ways to waste time because they need the stimulus of a deadline. Anything can become a distraction. They'll stop and read a cereal box if they happen across it. But in their case, the actual typing or drawing or whatever is the tip of the iceberg. Much of the work has gone on in their heads during those periods where they don't appear to be doing anything (not anything billable, anyway).

If your D answers were combined with As, you probably see yourself as the fount of ideas from which a successful business will spring. Maybe you can be the creative figurehead you imagine. You will, however, need someone more practical to run the company—someone who appreciates that even when you don't look like you're doing anything, you are. You are, aren't you? Partner yourself with a B and continually heap him or her with praise and money so there won't be any festering resentment.

If your D answers were combined with Bs, you can probably go it on your own. Once you have deadlines imposing some kind of discipline on you, there's no end to what you can accomplish. And with the organizational sense that your B side contributes, you probably have the combination of vision and practicality to get a successful enterprise going. You should probably feed that B side by taking courses in a few business disciplines.

If you ended up with Ds and a lot of Cs, you're probably better off with a real job that exploits your ability to get happily lost in a world of detail. You're probably not wildly ambitious, so if you find the right position and the right environment, you can enjoy the work for its own sake.

PLANNING YOUR OWN BUSINESS

So, you're an A with C rising, or D and A combination and you're going to pursue your dream. Don't just jump right in. If you can give yourself some time, you can make everything go more smoothly down the road. And maybe you can even do a lot of the preparatory work while you're still enjoying a paycheque. You might as well get used to working double shifts now.

Don't Throw Out the Baby with the Bath Water

Every business starts with an idea, but no matter how brilliant that idea may be, if it's in a field you know nothing about, don't take a flyer on it. You'll have too much to learn and not enough time to learn it.

Your knowledge and expertise are your most important assets, so don't toss them away as you chase after a new experience. A lot of creative people fall into this trap, especially those who get bored easily. They're not untalented or dimwitted—quite the opposite. It's just that once they've mastered something it no longer intrigues them, so they're off. And every time they move on they have to start over. But the same way you build your investments through the routine and mundane, you build your own market value through the incremental learning that has brought you to this point.

Where do you have experience? What are you good at? What are you bad at? Where will you need help? If you're an accountant and you want to start your own accounting firm, or take the training and become a financial planner, or design some new accounting software for a field you've worked in, or even become a cabinetmaker because it's been your hobby for 20 years, great. You're building on the skills and knowledge you already have. If you're an accountant and you want to be a lion tamer . . . well, as I recall, that guy's career counsellor suggested he start in banking and work up to lion taming from there. Expand on what you know. That's what pays off big time, whether you're changing jobs or careers or starting a business.

The only exception to this is when you're buying a franchise, because you're given a good template to work from and you have the support and training of a larger organization. Basically what you're buying *is* experience. The major consideration with a franchise is determining whether or not the numbers work. Look them over carefully, preferably with someone who's familiar with the market and the location.

Build Some Reserves

Before you go into business, spend some time stockpiling, especially if you're not going to get a package. Make sure you're in a strong position to leave your job. Some people have lost their homes and even their families because of the financial fallout of following their bliss.

Keep in mind when starting your own business that it takes time to make it successful. If you break even in three years it's exceptional. Most businesses (the ones that survive) start to take off only after five years. Five lean years. When I started I remember working seven days a week, 14 hours a day. In the beginning of my fifth year I did a quick calculation and realized that if I worked for someone else I'd be making a lot more per hour than I was on my own. It was a bit depressing, but I promised myself I'd give it 100% for one more year, and that's when the quantum leap happened. All of the good work, the experience and the contacts came together. Other business people tell me the same thing: often it's the fifth year where magic happens. That's not to say it can't happen sooner, but plan to live on less for five years.

It's difficult to make the transition if you're used to a good pay-cheque from an employer. Before you start a business, you should save enough money to live on for one year so you can cover your needs as you go through the start-up phase. You will likely be pouring a lot of your earnings back into the business and paying yourself a fairly skimpy salary so you might need to augment it. Max out your RRSP now—it's pre-tax money and it earns you a refund which you can also save. Later, if you need to borrow money from your RRSP to live on, you can do it without a terrific penalty because you will be in a low tax bracket. You probably won't be able to max out your RRSP for a few years *after* you start your business. You'll be investing in yourself instead and building up your carry-forward.

Starting now, learn to live on less so it doesn't come as a big shock when it happens. Take another look at your Cash Flow Statement and try to eliminate or cut back on anything that's not a necessity.

Make sure your credit rating is good, and if it's not, see what you can do to fix it.

Arm Yourself with Knowledge

Take classes. Join organizations. Talk to people in the field. Read books. Subscribe to trade publications. Download information off the Internet. Get a mentor who's done it before. Learn everything you can about the field you're going into. But equally important, learn everything you can about running a business. A lot of hardworking people with wonderful ideas have failed because they didn't have the fundamental business skills. You don't have to become an MBA. There are marvellous night school courses that teach everything you need to know about setting up and running a business, and often there are courses that deal with specific types of business. I can guarantee that you'll come away amazed at how much you didn't know.

If you're not good at running your personal finances, don't think things are going to be any better when you're in business. It's especially important to learn the basics of bookkeeping, taxation, maintaining cash flow and making projections. This won't eliminate the need for an accountant, but at least you'll be able to keep continuous tabs on what's happening with your company's money, and you'll be able to understand what the accountant is telling you.

I'm not suggesting that you do this all at once before you start your business. I've seen people who spend all their time educating themselves and not enough time doing the actual work that brings in the revenues. Education is a continual process.

Choose Your Partner(s) Carefully

If you function better with other people than alone, a partnership is worth considering. Having a partner means there is someone who cares about the business as much as you do. A partner can fill in the gaps in your skills and provide another perspective. So the first rule is don't have a partner who's just like you. Two people ought to mean twice the skills and range. Choose someone with complementary skills—and appreciate your differences. One's good at marketing, the other's good at managing. One's good at making deals, the other at making widgets. Allocate different responsibilities and respect the boundaries. Good partners share their strengths. I've seen any number of partners operate, and of course they have clashes, but when something contentious comes up, the successful ones always go back to whose department it is.

Having separate areas of responsibility does not mean that one partner gives up financial control. Partners have stolen from partners in the past. Even if one is the CFO, the other must be involved in most financial decisions and must have access to the books. From the start you need to agree on how often to get together to discuss the company's financial status, and how to share the responsibility for making decisions involving money.

That said, you'll be much happier if you share the same values. If one of you likes working hard and being on time and the other can't be counted on to do either, there'll be fireworks. Before you commit to each other (and yes, a partnership is very much like a marriage in many ways), get together and honestly discuss both your practical skills and your attitudes toward work and life—strengths and weaknesses. You have to respect each other or it won't work well. A Saver can work with a Spender if both are aware of the difference and agree to a few compromises, but if the difference comes as a horrible surprise and isn't dealt with, it can cause the kind of low-level stress that makes people go postal. Starting a business will provide all the stress you can possibly handle. You don't need the added aggravation of a partner who drives you nuts.

You'll be taking a smaller chance if you link up with someone you've seen operate—someone you've worked with before or dealt with on the job. Friends don't qualify unless they're friends with whom you've worked well in the past. If they're just people you like socially, you might not be friends for long.

Often, out of loyalty, people go into business with someone who helped come up with the original idea, and then find out that the idea is all that person's good for. The idea is the fun part. It's not a business until a lot of very hard work goes into it, and the person you choose as your partner has to be as capable of work as you are. If the idea you want to pursue was somebody else's brainchild, but that somebody isn't partner material, you have to be willing to give up the idea. Say you don't think it's big enough for two people and you'd like to follow up on it, but if that person wants to do it, you'll back off. Then, alas, if they say they want to go with it, back off (even though you know you could do it 10 times better).

The most difficult partnership of all is three. I'm not saying a triumvirate can't work, but I've seen more three-people partnerships go awry than any other combination. I'm not sure why—maybe it's just too easy for two to gang up on one. All I can say is, if there are going to be more than two partners, consider moving up to four.

Have a Plan

If you go into business, you have to know what you're doing. Literally. What exactly are you providing to customers? What are your goals? What steps will you take to reach them? How long will each step take? Knowing what you're doing involves clarifying your ideas and defining what you want to accomplish.

Anybody who's going to give you any money is going to ask to see a business plan. It consists of a description of your business, a marketing plan, a financial plan and a management plan. Even if you're not borrowing to start your business, you should invest the time in writing a business

PETER CREATES A BUSINESS PLAN

Peter has developed a process that makes the plastic in old computer casings reusable, and he wants to use his process as the basis of a business that recycles old computers. His statements might look like this.

Vision—I want to cut down on the number of old computers going into the landfill by turning their plastic casings into a material that can be reused, and by recycling other reusable parts.

Mission Statement—My company will collect obsolete computers from the Tri-Regions area, convert used computer casing plastic into recycled material suitable for new casings, and reclaim the raw materials from other computer parts to sell to hardware manufacturers.

Objectives—Improve reclamation rate by making computer owners think of my company before they throw out computers. Manufacture a recycled plastic considered as good as new, which can under-price new materials. Extract raw materials as economically as possible for resale. Consistently increase demand for recycled materials among computer manufacturers

Goals—Institute drop-off depots and pick-up service within Tri-Regions area. Form strategic alliances with city and environmental organizations that can promote depots and pick-ups. Analyze the most cost-effective ways of using paid advertising. Locate larger space for plant.

Time—Get six institutional or corporate customers within six months. Be the subject of articles in trade publications and local media within first year. Hire two new salespeople within first year. Move to larger space within two years.

plan. It's an exercise that makes you deal with myriad details before they deal with you—everything from who are your customers, to what salaries and benefits you will offer employees, to what kind of accounting system you plan to use. You can find excellent business plan templates in books, software and Web sites.

The Mission-Objectives-Goals process is a helpful first step before you write your business plan. It's a classic formula, used by everybody from the biggest multinationals on down, and it goes like this:

1. **Vision**—define your dream in writing.

2. **Mission Statement**—convert your vision into a clear statement of intent.

3. **Objectives**—identify key objectives (*i.e.*, aims, strategic positions you want to attain).

4. **Goals**—create a list of specific tasks that will lead you to your objectives.

5. **Time**—assign a projected time or date to complete each task.

This exercise of defining and refining is best done with more than one brain. A consultant helps (with this and many other steps), or a trusted business associate, or the group of people who will be creating the organization. If the process is new to you, you would definitely benefit from the contributions of someone who's been through it before. Expect to spend between one and two days. This may seem like a waste of time when you've got a million other things to do, but in business as in your personal life, you can't get to where you're going if you don't know where it is.

As your business grows and changes, and often before your business even gets off the ground, you will occasionally need to take time from your harried day-to-day work to look once more at the big picture and see where your list and business plan need revision. As the real world makes its demands you will probably rework all of this many times. But at least you're changing within a structured way of thinking, instead of just reacting to circumstances.

RUNNING YOUR BUSINESS

In theory, there is no difference between theory and practice.
In practice, there is. — Chuck Reid

Running your own business has a lot of bonuses, but don't ever fool yourself that one of them is working less. You will labour harder at this than you have ever worked at anything in your life. I've not met a single entrepreneur who didn't comment on the astonishing workload. One acquaintance, who started a specialty catering service with her sister, told me that there were times when the two of them came home so fatigued after solid weeks of 14-hour days that they both found themselves weeping as they walked through the door. However, after just a few moments of thought, would they rather go back to working for someone else? Never in a million years. They realized they were building and developing something all their own and doing it their way; they would never have worked that hard for anyone but themselves. After two-and-a-half years, they are just now starting to take two days off a week.

That's the thing about going out on your own—when you're working late it's not because someone made you—it's because you're on a roll, or you have a deadline. You have the flexibility that comes when no one's looking over your shoulder. There is only your client and yourself to answer to (mind you, clients *are* your boss). The work feels different because you know that you'll reap whatever rewards are to come. And the rewards can be glorious. When things go well, you get the accolades, the money, the glow of accomplishment. You have built something worthwhile.

Stay Focused

In the flurry of decisions that surrounds the entrepreneur, probably the most important is how to allocate your time. Even if you're a sole proprietor, you might have to hire help sometimes. Know what are you good at, what's productive for you, what your strengths are. Identify your weaknesses too, but don't work too hard on improving them. You'll just end up with strong weaknesses. Say you have trouble communicating with staff because you talk too quickly and don't like to tell anyone anything more than once (which sounds awfully like me, come to think of it). You could work hard at it and get better—but you'll never be great at it, so why waste the time? Rather than doing a half-baked job yourself, maybe you're better to communicate with one person who has the skill and patience to inform and teach the rest of the staff on your behalf. Do what you do best and whenever possible hire other people to do what you don't do well.

When you do hire others, be organized and use their billable hours prudently. Can you afford to pay your accountant to organize the shoebox full of travel receipts? A few paper clips and the most primitive of filing systems could have saved you hundreds of dollars. And if you're incapable of even that degree of structure, you need to hire someone to organize you. Without that kind of help you will forever be searching the piles on your desk for a lost document or checking under the couch cushions for your cell phone instead of nailing down a million dollar contract.

Avoid time-wasters. Always be on top of your billings and collections so you can see if any clients are lax in their payments. You have to be a bit hard hearted, but if someone hasn't paid you for a few months, you might never get paid. You're better to stop working for them before it's too late.

The same is true for clients who demand a great deal more than you're contracted to deliver. It's an odd thing, but often the people who are getting the best deals are the most demanding and difficult. If you can't please them, fire them. Nicely suggest that they might be better off with one of your competitors (thereby killing two birds with one stone).

When you're going after contracts, listen to your instincts. Does your gut tell you the deadline is undoable or that you can't provide what they're asking for without taking a loss? It's tough to be tough when you don't know where your next job is coming from, but remember, if you take that dubious job you may not survive financially until a better job comes along.

Another big time waster is busy work. And, oh, isn't it tempting to clean up your hard drive when you really ought to be writing that proposal for the Snarfley contract? One of the most talented and hardworking people I know is always ensnared in busy work. Ask him to do something for you and he'll get on it immediately. In the meantime, anything he has to do for his own business gets put off or relegated to nights and weekends. Know the difference between the work you have to do and work you're doing to avoid the work you have to do.

Finally, don't panic and don't get discouraged just because things are proceeding slowly. Even if you've got a good idea and you see it building, the rewards don't come immediately. In my early days, I'd get a new client every now and then, but I couldn't get excited because I'd worry where the next one was coming from. It's not just you. Everyone feels worried and even down sometimes, but don't let those feelings rule you. Keep reminding yourself that if you just keep on working and building, everything will eventually pick up. Remember, if it were easy, everyone would be doing it. Success is often built on doing the work others are unwilling to do. Not letting yourself get down is one component of that precious commodity, self-discipline.

Get Insured

Apart from the usual insurance on property and life, there are a few other types that make good sense for business owners. The first is disability. If something happens to you when you're working for yourself or with a partner, you not only need to have an alternative income while you're out of commission, you need to replace yourself to keep the business running. In case one partner becomes permanently disabled, you might look at purchasing disability buyout insurance, which will allow one partner to buy out the other. It's quite expensive, but worth taking a look at.

By the same token, you need to insure for employees who have a ton of knowledge or expertise. Sometimes these key people die, taking a great deal of valuable information with them in their heads. In the worst case, such a loss can destroy a company that was built around the developments of the person who died: the engineer who invented the new fibre optic switch, or the programmer who was working on the revolutionary procurement software.

If you're in a partnership, don't neglect to arrange buy-sell agreements. Jimmy and June are partners in a $5 million import-export business, and when June dies, her half of the business goes to her husband, Buddy. Jimmy and Buddy have always merely tolerated each other because of the business, but there's no way they're going to succeed as partners. Buy-sell insurance will cover the cost of Jimmy buying out Buddy.

Protect Yourself

Most fraud comes from within the organization so if you don't set up good checks and balances you leave yourself vulnerable. People, including your employees, can be easily tempted. Just ask the stockroom supervisor when September rolls around. Suddenly there's a mysterious run on pens, paper, steno pads and anything else that could be pressed into business as school supplies. And that's the very least that can happen. You can't stay on top of everything, so it's worthwhile to set up systems that take care of themselves as much as possible. No system is infallible, and some fraud and theft, unfortunately, is inevitable. But a system can keep you from turning into a paranoid ogre and get on with running your business.

Live on Less

In the beginning, you'll just have to get used to it—there won't be as much money coming in, and what does come in might be in spurts. It will take discipline to live on an irregular income, but you can do it. Go back to Chapter 5, Getting On Track. Pay yourself what you have calculated as your absolute rock-bottom necessities and consider everything else extra.

We're talking food, mortgage, basic clothing, transportation, insurance—period. When you're starting a business, your needs don't even include contributions to your RRSPs or savings. You can build those later.

Set up separate bank accounts for your needs and put everything else in a savings account. If there's no money coming in, you can draw money from the savings account until the cash flow picks up. If after a year you can cover your needs and have some money in your savings account, then you can contribute to RRSPs or take a vacation. You may even be able to give yourself a raise.

Spread the Tax Savings

One of the biggest bonuses of starting a business is the tax savings. The corporate tax rate is much lower than the personal tax rate and there are many ways to reduce the amount of tax you have to pay. One of them is to split income among family members. Pay your kids to come in and do the cleaning rather than hiring someone else to do it. Use your spouse's skills, and pay for them. The business will be paying and reaping the benefits of the services, the family will be getting the money and in all likelihood paying lower taxes than if you just paid yourself all that money. This plan is especially beneficial if you're starting out on a shoestring and can't pay yourself very much.

Incorporate When You're Ready

One of the biggest questions I hear from people who start businesses is "should I incorporate?"

Ask yourself this question: if you falter, will you be leaving yourself open to lawsuits? In other words, will other people or companies spend money and time on your behalf in the expectation that they will be paid, or that you will perform on their behalf? If you fail to pay them or perform as you have promised, they can sue you. If you're not incorporated, they can sue you personally, taking your house and possessions as well as the assets of your business. If you are incorporated, they can only sue you for the assets of your business.

Once your business has grown to the point that it covers more than your personal needs, it's definitely time to incorporate. The company is taxed at a lower rate than you are personally, so once you've paid yourself, there's more money available in the company to help it grow. Often in a new business the cash flow is erratic, but if all the money goes into the company, the company can pay you a stable salary.

Be a Good Partner

Partners complain about each other. Partners vent their frustrations with each other. It's all part of being a partner. When one of them does it in my office, I interject a gentle reminder that each of them contributes in a different way. Sometimes one contributes more than the other, and then the trend reverses. There are ebbs and flows. This is where you have to use all your communication skills. If you don't like what the other person is doing, don't just say that you don't like it—you'd better have an alternative. If you don't have a better solution yourself, you might need to bring in outside help.

Ask yourself, am I being a good partner? Being a good partner is as hard as the actual work you do. Try to remember your different roles and everything your partner does for the company. It's a universal human truth that nobody else's job seems as difficult or frustrating or time-consuming as one's own. If you chose well, you can trust this person to be working hard, even out of your sight. This is someone who has as much riding on the success of the company as you do.

Provide Great Client Service

Your clients hire you to take care of their interests. It's not always easy. If you don't have their ear you're wasting words. Sometimes people think they're far too busy to speak to you, even though you can tell them something that will save them money or trouble. If you're in business for yourself, remind yourself how busy *you* are and how few of the communications actually filter up to you. If an associate calls with important information about your security or future, don't you want to know?

Keep in touch with your clients. Ask if there are any problems and find out if they see any future problems that need to be cut off at the pass. A bonus of keeping up-to-date is that you learn of glitches immediately. Solve them immediately and you've gained a client for life. Say someone is in a partnership and really ought to have a buy-sell agreement—it's my job to keep them up-to-date. If they won't talk to me, I'll keep at them until they do because I believe it's important for them. When I call a client, I ask, "Do you have a minute to talk?," thereby asking permission to take some of their time. If they're not open to listening, I'm wasting my time and theirs. They won't thank me for disturbing them, but I can be forgiven for intruding. If they have a moment and I can suggest something that will save them money, time or trouble, I have a client for life. It's up to me to do my part of the job, and the ultimate job is to make life easier for the client.

Another part of that is delivering on your commitments. Simply put, don't make promises you can't keep. Though you might look good by saying that you'll have something completed long before anyone else could possibly do it, you'll look bad if you're late (for an unrealistic deadline). Going back to the client to ask for more time or more money makes you look unprofessional, so you have to learn to project realistic timelines and budgets. Experience is a big help here, and if you don't have it yourself, find someone who does to look over your proposals or proposed deals. An experienced hand can save your butt by pointing out that you haven't budgeted for overtime due to weather delays, or you've failed to build in time for the client to meet on and approve each step of the project. Meanwhile, for future reference, keep careful track of how much time and money each step in a project takes so that eventually you can project with confidence.

Your best bet is to overestimate the time a project will take, then if you come in early or under budget, you'll look like a hero.

THE FAMILY BUSINESS

What could be better than working with someone who knows you so well that you can finish each other's sentences? Someone you've shared life with since you were in diapers. Someone you can fight with without fearing it will lead to a terrible rift. Someone you can always trust.

And what could be worse than being in business with someone who knows exactly how to drive you out of your mind? Someone who will never be able to appreciate that you're an adult now. Someone you can fight with at the drop of a hat. Someone you can always trust to do the same annoying thing over and over.

Hmm. I guess it's no wonder that most family businesses don't survive through the third generation.

An absolute essential for any family business is a board made up of people from outside the family who can give dispassionate advice. They might have to go with one faction in a family dispute or make the tough decision that everybody's been avoiding because it will hurt someone's feelings, so they must be known to be impartial. Choose people whose businesses are the next step up from yours. They've seen and dealt with the problems already.

Relatives Building a Business

There are two kinds of family businesses. The first is when relatives, be they siblings, cousins or parent and child, build a business from the ground up. As with partners, this setup works best when the relatives have different skills and take charge of different aspects of the business. It will make everything easier if you assign different responsibilities based on your unique abilities, and then try not to step on each other's feet. Businesses bloom when you appreciate each other's strengths and contributions.

On the other hand, don't become insular just because you're family—that's all the more reason to hire outside expertise or ask the opinions of others. If you're good at the same thing and you believe that two, three or four minds are better than one, you may have found an alternative avenue to success. Just be sure that there is a person on board handling the things that you and your relatives don't—a business manager, marketing manager, factory supervisor, systems analyst—whatever you need. Your big success will come from determining where you need help and hiring it.

The section in this chapter on partnerships (page 150) applies whether you're strangers or relatives. As to any longstanding resentments ("she dropped a balloon full of paint on my head when I was trying to impress that girl I'd been fantasizing about!!"), get a therapist. I'm serious. The emotional component of your business will be deeper than that of most business partners, and if that becomes a problem, understand that it is emotion, not reason that is driving in the wedge. This is business. It's why you should have an arm's-length board to guide you.

Passing on a Family Business

The other kind of family business is the one where the business is already established and now there's another generation coming up. This one can be fraught with even more problems because it involves senior family members who have built something and a younger generation that either expects something or bears the weight of expectations. Do any of the following sound familiar?

- "You were never there when I was growing up. Why should I care about your business now?"
- "Dad always wanted me to go into business with him. How can I tell him that I want to be a cellist?"
- "Well, if it's what Mom wants, I guess that's fine with me."

- "Dad and Uncle Harvey picked you just because you're the oldest!"
- "You're squeezing me out because your mother never liked my father!"
- "You don't care a bit about Mom's business. You're just doing it because it'll be easy!"

I could go on. There's nothing like a nice juicy, profitable business to divide a family. Over the years I have seen a few ideas that help families overcome the hurdles they put in their own way.

Don't Assume

Just because you have poured your heart and soul into a business, don't expect that your children will do the same. Your children are not you. Have you ever asked them what they want, or have you just assumed that they would follow your lead? They may have their own ideas about their future, or they may want nothing else but to build on what you have created.

Don't depend on having the next generation follow you into the business. Remember that there are a number of ways of following in your path. Your kids, nephews or nieces may want to start their own businesses, just the way you did. They may want to join your firm and take over a position—not necessarily yours—or they may want to go off in directions that you never imagined. You won't be able to force anybody into doing anything except by emotional blackmail, and is that worth the trouble? Let them know that if they ever start their own business, no matter what it is (excepting something you are morally opposed to) you will help them with business advice. I've found that when two generations find any kind of common ground, relations become a whole lot easier.

There's one sure way of finding out just what the next generation wants. Ask. Ask in a way that doesn't assume anything or put any pressure on. If they exhibit any reluctance or anxiety, let them follow their own muse. Maybe at some point they'll come back. If not, they're on their own and that's the way they wanted it to be. Not your problem.

Bring Them in Properly

If the kids do want to join the family firm, you have to be careful how you bring them in. It's helpful if they work in a few other places first so they can get some experience in the world beyond your company. This move will give them the needed perspective when they take over from you.

They should also work in a number of capacities once they come to work for you. They'll learn the business as thoroughly as you know it, and you'll get a chance to evaluate their skills and determine where they eventually belong in the company. Besides, they have to pay their dues. To bring them in at the top is to create resentments among other employees, and to install them in positions they're not suited for is doing a disservice to the company.

Treat Them Fairly

Sometimes equal isn't fair. If one family member has worked longer in the business and contributed more, then that person may have earned a bigger slice of the business. Siblings who haven't worked in the business may get equal shares of the assets outside the business, or a child who is disabled may need more of an inheritance to make life comfortable.

Plan a Smooth Transition

In my dealings with family businesses, one issue comes up time and time again and that is the transition from one generation to the next. Dad hates to let go. He built it; it's his. The kids are ready to take over but don't want to look like they're pushing him out. So Dad just keeps on coming in every day, figuring when the kids are ready for him to leave, they'll tell him. Meanwhile he's in control and the "kids," now twice the age he was when he started the business, don't know how to tell him to retire.

Most of this frustration and resentment can be avoided when the elder of the business takes the lead in handing over the reins.

Parents, especially Givers, should be careful to get fair market value for the business when they pass it on. A friend of a friend decided to give his business to his children and just take a salary. With inflation, his salary wasn't enough, so he asked the kids for a raise, but they wouldn't give it to him.

Estate planning is the second part of the transition, whether or not the kids are involved in the company. This can be a particularly touchy subject because the children are often unwilling to bring up the subject for fear of looking as if they're just waiting for Mom or Dad to die. Again, it's up to the elders to find out what everyone wants and to make the decisions. The best idea I've ever seen is for the parents to go away with the children for a weekend without any spouses. The parents ask what the kids would like to have happen when Mom and Dad are no longer around. No decisions are made during this weekend. It's just a time for discussion. Then Mom and Dad get back to the kids later when they've made up their minds about what to do. Do this before it needs to be done—before anyone is sick or in failing health—so the discussion does not have to take place under an awful shadow.

Families dealing with these issues often think that their situation is unique, but these dynamics happen in almost all family businesses. The line between business and personal gets smudged because you are a family. Sometimes it's just easier to fall back on old habits—relatives know which buttons to push, and old habits die hard. On the other hand, there's nothing better than knowing someone so well. When everyone works together, the success can be unbelievable. The Canadian Association of Family Enterprise (**www.cafenational.org**) has branches across the country and provides a wonderful forum for discussing the problems peculiar to family businesses.

CHANGING CAREERS

After all this, maybe it's clear to you that your own business isn't what you want. You're really just looking for a job that suits you better than the one you have. As usual, the first step is to identify what you want, and there are excellent books, and Web sites available, as well as career counsellors, workshops and vocational testing companies that can guide you on that fascinating personal journey.

When you are ready to change jobs or careers, make sure that you're in a good position to leave. If you can, start quietly looking while you're still employed. I say quietly because of stories of people who've posted their CV on the Internet, which has then been spotted by their current employers. End of current employment.

As with entrepreneurs, you should build some reserves, especially if you won't receive a package from your current job. If you will receive a package, watch out for the temptation to take a big break with the money. Take a couple of weeks, but then start looking for another job or building toward your new career. If you don't, you'll find the money will diminish at about the same rate as your self-confidence. Not only that, you may have to dip into your reserves or go into debt to stay afloat. As much as you have to have balance in your own life, remember what employers are looking for. They want keen people. If you've been off for a year, they're going to ask what you've been doing.

It seems we live with more interesting opportunities than ever before, and more possibilities of truly finding your place in the world of work. But even if you find the greatest job or start the most exciting business, the time will come for you to retire. In Chapter 11, you'll look at the third stage of life—a stage that is growing longer as we live longer. If you have Enough, it can be a time of great rewards.

I'VE GOT ENOUGH—NOW WHAT?

*Let this be an example for the acquisition of all knowledge,
virtue, and riches. By the fall of drops of water, by degrees,
a pot is filled. — The Hitopadesa (Fables and Proverbs
from the Sanskrit)*

Well, here we are, almost at the beginning. This whole book has been aimed at delivering you safely to a new place in your life, one where you get to decide how to spend your time and your money. Once you have Enough, you can retire. Sounds simple, doesn't it? Just stop working and start living on what you've saved and invested. Well, I hate to tell you, it can be seriously complicated, emotionally and financially. There's a big difference between anticipating your goal and achieving it. In this chapter, I'll help you identify the emotional and financial fallout of retirement, and steer you around some of the roadblocks. The object in both cases is to make sure you and your estate retain as much of what you've built up as possible.

RETIREMENT: THE EMOTIONAL SIDE

Most of the people I deal with retire and suddenly I can't see them for dust. They're outta there—going on cruises, fixing up the cabin, taking courses, bicycling around France, volunteering for charities, taking the grandkids out to the planetarium. They tell me they don't even remember how they fit work in before.

Part of their enjoyment comes from financial security, I'm sure; but on top of that it's the attitude. They know that work isn't who you are. It's a means to an end, and it can be challenging and fun, but it's not the sum total of you. These people have things they're interested in, new ideas and activities they want to explore, time to spend with people they love—and they're relishing it all.

You're Still the Same Old You

Once you've determined when you will be able to retire comfortably, you have to get comfortable with retirement. How you leave work behind depends on whether you're a Builder, a Spender, a Giver or a Saver.

Builders are often hooked on work for its own sake. Givers sometimes can't leave behind the co-workers or employees who depend on them. Spenders believe they're younger than they are and retirement can come as a shock. Savers can't believe they really truly have Enough.

DAVID WONDERS IF IT'S REALLY SAFE TO RETIRE

David was a Saver, born just on the tail-end of the Depression. He did well in his career, put his four wonderful kids through college, saved and invested well, yet enjoyed rewards along the way. He could retire tomorrow. In fact, he could have retired five years ago. But three times a year he comes in to talk to me, supposedly about his investments, but really just to assure himself that he truly does have Enough. During these sessions, I encourage him to let go. It has taken him longer than most to prepare, but finally he's emotionally ready. He has accepted that, yes, the money is there and he can start using it. Before he could give up working, he also had to know that he wasn't giving up his usefulness or his ability to earn (just in case I'd miscalculated), so he arranged to fill in when others were on vacation. Knowing that he could work if he wanted to was that little extra something he needed before he could make the break. I have a feeling he'll drop the work after a few times.

For each person, letting go is a different process. Even for people who have been eagerly anticipating their days of leisure, the reality can clash with their dreams. They haven't expected that they'll miss the camaraderie of the workplace, or the perks of their job, or just the feeling of being in the loop. They haven't realized that people will look at them differently now. And, let's face it, doesn't retiring mean the productive part of your life is over? That you've reached the point of no return?

It's easy to think that way if the only thing you've done to prepare yourself is say "Boy, I can't wait until I don't have to work anymore!"

Work can be a lot of stress and frustration, and it's fine to look forward to *not* doing something, but you should try to be looking forward to *doing* something too, otherwise you're gazing into a void.

Maybe that's why retirement comes as such a shock to some people: it's been their one and only goal, and once they reach it—now what? As a financial advisor I have been privy to the hopes and dreams of so many wonderful people. When they've achieved their goals, we've celebrated. Every now and then a client would die young, and I would feel devastated because I knew what was on their "unfinished" list. But in more recent years I asked myself, what if I died early? I realized that I hope to have a hundred unfinished goals, otherwise I'm dead on earth. You don't just sit around say "Okay, my goals are done: now I can stop living." You're more alive when you're aiming for something.

What Do You Want to Do?

In some European countries, when people are getting ready to retire, they work five days, then four, three, two, then one, slowly filling the days with other things to do. We don't do it that way, but it seems like such a good idea. Maybe, when we can't do it that way, we need to go back to setting goals. In those five years before you retire, incorporate new things you want to do into your yearly goals. If you've decided you want to grow your own vegetables, start reading up on the subject and visiting display gardens. Then you've initiated something that can continue after you've retired, so that you'll have something to look forward to.

If you have something major that you want to do when you retire, can you break it down and plan how you will get it done? If it's travel, well, what does that mean? Do you want to go on round-the-world cruises? On what? Luxury liners? Freighters? Banana boats? Which countries do you want to visit? Do you want to learn a bit of the language before you go? What do you want to do when you get there? Answering all these questions will give you projects to begin before you retire—and projects that can take up the slack after you retire.

Maybe your plan is to get involved in charity work, but if you haven't been involved before, how do you know what kind of work you want to do? Start looking at what you like to do best and where you think you could be the most help. Talk to volunteer agencies about what they need and see if there's anything that gets you excited. Start doing some work one or two evenings a week in the years before you retire, so you'll know if you want to get further involved when you have more time. Get specific. Try also to go beyond your major passion. Even the most fanatical golfer can't play golf all day every day. Maybe a good approach is to look at a variety of opportunities involving different combinations of mind, body, senses, spirit and community.

I read a study recently that found that retired people were the most content and happy with their lives. One of the things that made a real difference was planning their tasks for the day and then completing them, whether it was something as simple as taking out the garbage or as complicated as coordinating a fundraiser. A sense of accomplishment came from keeping their word to themselves.

Do the Most Ambitious Things First

Plan to do the stuff that takes the most energy when you're young. If you want to build a boat, go prospecting for gold or get a degree in medieval literature, you'll have more energy and stamina to do them soon after you retire. Leave the less ambitious things for later when you're older. You might not have the desire to hike up the Himalayas in your eighties, but you still might be able to learn the Goldberg Variations on the harpsichord.

Be Patient with Each Other

One of the little shocks for couples is suddenly being together all the time. Your financial attitudes won't magically change on retirement. Any incompatibilities could well be amplified because your resources are now finite. I know lots of Savers who continue to put away part of their monthly income, and who build up thousands of dollars in savings accounts. It doesn't matter that the money is losing ground to inflation, or that they already have Enough and could easily be enjoying their entire income. What matters is that they need a cushion or they don't feel safe. They drive their spouses and children batty.

I've seen Builders who keep wanting to take it to the edge—using their retirement money—and others who start spending madly on their collections or fascinations now that they have more time to devote to them. Spenders can feel deeply thwarted by the thought of never having more income than they have now, and unless there are a few spending sprees built into the budget, they might cut loose. Givers—oh, dear— Givers can be the worst of all in retirement. They misinterpret Enough to mean Enough for Everybody, and as well as having family to help out, they're the target of every charity in the phone book.

GARTH GIVES IT ALL AWAY

Garth was retired and had recently hit it big with stocks in a dot.com company. A Giver if there ever was one, he wanted to help out his son, who was starting a business. Garth didn't want to cash in the shares because he thought he'd have to pay too much tax, so instead he used his dot.com shares as collateral for a loan. The bank, having walked down this road many times, demanded a personal guarantee. Garth never gave it any thought because these shares made him rich on paper. Alas, the son wasn't much of a entrepreneur. He went under and unfortunately, so did the dot.com Garth was using as collateral. When the bank went after Garth, he lost just about everything. At a time when he should have been on Easy Street, he had to start over.

Now might be a good time to go back to your Goals and wish lists from Chapter 3. An understanding of each other's impulses and urges will help you plan how to use your retirement income in a way that makes both of you comfortable. Don't worry. It might take a whole year to learn to handle this new intimacy.

Finish Up at Work

How many movies have we seen about the old detective who has one unsolved case that he just can't put away? If you want to close the file on some things before you leave, put those on your list and make sure you get them done, or at least well underway for other people to take over, so that you're emotionally prepared to move on when the time comes.

If your work truly is your passion, and you can't find anything that will give you the same buzz (you're a Builder, aren't you?), do what David did and consider a part-time job, either at the firm you work for now or at another one. Volunteer work or mentoring can fill that gap too, or you might even want to hang out your shingle as a consultant. A mostly retired colleague of mine has set up a home office. It's his sanctum sanctorum, filled with business stuff, a couple of file cabinets, two computers, etc. He has found this a useful bridge into retirement because he still has somewhere to go every morning, and things to do. Sounds like a great idea. Hey, the kids are gone anyway. There should be a room or two available.

Sometimes the only thing that can help people give up working is knowing they can work, even though they don't have to. I've met a former police chief who was driving a bus and having the time of his life. I've also met a high-powered executive who'd retired and taken a job as a courier. Both of them had pensions, but they just wanted to do something they thought was fun.

There's an interesting flip side to this idea. When people know they have enough money to retire on if they have to, they start enjoying their work more. They've been worried about being laid off, or they're finding the job demands winding them too tight, or they've been promoted beyond the part of their work that attracted them in the first place. But as soon as they have the bare minimum that they can retire on, they lighten up considerably. Even if their retirement income would be quite a comedown, just knowing they could survive on it frees them, because now everything else is gravy. At that stage people will often quit their high-powered job and get another job doing just what they like, or they'll start ignoring the negative parts of their job and enjoy the positive. It's a wonderful thing to see.

This whole process of thinking about what you want to do when you retire starts well before you actually retire. Give it five years at least—and enjoy the process.

RETIREMENT: THE FINANCIAL SIDE

The best gift to your children is not to be dependent on them.

Here it comes again. *Get good advice.* Even if all you will have is a company pension, government pensions and some extra savings, a financial planner can help you get everything in order, so you can save as much tax and make as much from your investments as possible when you start drawing an income. And believe me, the more you have, the more complicated everything gets because of tax issues. Do you use your RRSP money first? Do you use non-registered money first? What do you use your non-registered money for? Should you buy a RRIF or an annuity? How do your pensions fit into the whole scheme of things? Where can you save on tax? How much money will you have: how much are you going to spend; what do you want to spend the money on?

To you it might be overwhelming, but a good financial planner does this stuff every day. Everybody's situation is different. Give your financial

Marjorie Gets a Second Opinion

My client Marjorie was a widow. She and her husband had always lived a very wealthy life, and she was used to spending whatever she wanted, which wasn't hard because she was a Spender and a Giver by nature. Her husband was still working when he died—because he loved his work, she thought, but really because he had to. When he died, she kept on spending, and the stockbroker who was advising her told her that was just fine. So she was living as she always had, and giving a lot of money to her children, who had all come to expect regular infusions of cash.

Somehow Marjorie had a sense that she should cut down a bit, and she came to me for a second opinion. She was right. It turned out that she was going to run out of money if she didn't cut back. The stockbroker was quite young and, I suspect, thought Marjorie was pretty old and didn't have long to go. They had never sat down and done a financial plan. Fifteen years later Marjorie's still doing fine, although she's been forced to restrict her spending and tell her children that they'll have to get along without the extras she'd been providing. To her, those have been small sacrifices in exchange for knowing she'll be able to take care of herself.

planner every bit of information you have: the roof is going to need replacing in two years; there's a family reunion coming up in Belgium; you plan to buy an RV; you'll be getting a lump sum from your employer; you have some revenue property you plan to sell . . . They're all pieces of the puzzle your financial planner will need to put together to build your financial picture. The government has figured out innumerable ways to get money out of you, but also given you innumerable ways to keep it. Your financial advisor will help you keep whatever you can and make the most out of whatever you have.

WHAT HAPPENS WHEN YOU RETIRE?

Depends on when you do it. Read on.

Early Retirement

If you have the money to retire at age 55, or even 25 for that matter, you can start withdrawing income from your RRSP and paying tax on it. If you don't have a company pension coming to you or you're not independently wealthy, I'll assume you've run your numbers and you know you can retire at this age without having to sit on the street with a cup in 10 years. If you haven't run the numbers, go back to the beginning of the book and start over.

For some people, the decision isn't that clear-cut. They've been offered an early retirement package by their employer, and the lump sum looks tempting. How much will it cost to replace the benefits they might lose, like life insurance, medical or dental coverage, CPP contributions or a company car? How much of the package can be rolled into an RRSP? How much will they have to live on if they take the package? Are they still young enough to find other work? If you're pondering an early retirement package, know your Enough number and check out the terms with a financial advisor who can take all these factors into account.

When you decide to take early retirement from a company, your pension will be less than what you would earn at 65, but you're getting to spend all those extra years doing what you want. For a lot of people, less income is a great trade-off for more years of leisure.

The same is true of your CPP (Canada Pension Plan). From age 60 to 65, it's possible to take a reduced CPP every month if you're making less than a minimal-earned income (approximately $6,000 annually at this point). If, at any time during that period, you haven't worked for a full year, you can start taking your reduced CPP. Take it early if you can. Waiting for five years will give you a little bit more money per month, but in the meantime you could have been collecting for five years. If you start taking your CPP at 60, you'll be 77 before that difference evens out. I remember a client of mine floundering about as she tried to decide whether to take less money at 60 or more at 65. Her reason was that she might live as long as her dad, who was 90 at that point. Then she screwed up her face for a moment and said, "What the heck? He's been sitting in a chair for the last 10 years." She took it at 60. My advice is to do the same.

If you're expecting a company pension but can't collect it until later, now is probably the time to use some of your RRSP as income. If that's your only income, you control what tax bracket you're in by keeping what you take within certain limits. When you're older and your company pension and Old Age Security kick in, you can start taking less from your RRSP. Another way of providing income is to use non-RRSP funds to purchase a term-certain annuity. Most people when speaking about an annuity think of something that lasts for life. Here we're discussing annuities that begin and end within a certain period of time. The minimum time frame for a term-certain annuity is five years, but it can also be substantially longer. There are some tax advantages in using annuities as a bridge, and they're worth discussing with your advisor to see if they're applicable to you.

If you're planning to retire early, make sure you have enough money to provide for those things you might want or need later on, like travel, education, home improvement or possibly long-term care. Your wish list and Yearly Goals from Chapter 3 will help you plan. And I suggest that you take a look at your parents and see what they're going through now, or anticipating. Believe it or not, this could happen to you too.

Age 65

On your sixty-fifth birthday, Canada Customs and Revenue Agency is at your door—this time, to give you money (so don't get too feisty with them). That's when you have to start taking your Canada Pension Plan and Old Age Security. It's even a good idea to apply for them a couple of months in advance, because you will have to wait before you start receiving them.

Canada Pension Plan is the government retirement plan for people who have worked. You and your employer have contributed a specific amount based on your income, and you will receive a monthly pension based on your working income (self-employed people pay double because they're both employee and employer). As I write, the maximum is about $900 per month. Your contributions now are paying the people who are already retired. Your own CPP will come out of the contributions of the people who are working when you're retired. However, unlike a company pension plan or your RRSP, there is no actual pool of capital being invested. Your current contributions are funding current retirees, hence the fear that there won't be enough when all the Baby Boomers retire.

If one spouse was never employed, or wasn't employed for as many years, that person will earn less from CPP. You can then split your CPP benefit equally once you're both 65, which may mean more money in your pockets. For instance, if I get $900 and my husband gets $300, I give him $450 and he gives me $150 so we both declare $600 a month in CPP benefits. He's in a low tax bracket because he's not earning much from his RRSP, so we end up saving income tax. I would go back to receiving my $900 per month if my husband predeceased me. When one spouse dies, the CPP goes back to the way it was originally. To get this benefit, apply to the CPP office a couple of months before you reach 65.

Old Age Security is paid to everyone, regardless of work history. If you're earning over a certain amount in retirement income, currently over $53,000, the government can take back all or a portion of your OAS income, referred to a claw-back.

Oh, and I do hope they change the name Old Age Security someday. Old people are a lot younger longer than they used to be. How about "Senior Security?"

Company Pension or superannuation will provide an income for life, and sometimes beyond. If the income is indexed, it will increase as inflation goes up. If not, you will feel a pinch in times of high inflation because you'll be receiving the same income as you did when inflation was low.

These private pension plans give you choices on how to take the income. If you take the income only for your life, your income will be greater than if you want your spouse to continue receiving it after you die. You can also choose to leave the income to your estate if both you and your spouse die. Usually when you near retirement your company will give you a list of options which you may want to take to your financial advisor to discuss. Look at the options very carefully.

There are a number of considerations when deciding on your best course of action. Do you both have pensions and/or savings that will provide a comfortable monthly income? If so, you might as well enjoy the greater income because your spouse won't need it.

Is there a big gap in your ages? A joint and last survivor benefit, that is, to have your spouse continue to collect your pension after you die, might not be worthwhile if the man is a lot older than the woman. Then, the statistics say that the woman is likely to go on collecting for a good while after the man is gone, so the pension company will reduce your monthly income to make up for that likelihood. For example, let's say Richard is 65 and Linda is 55. Linda is already considered seven years younger than Richard because women tend to live seven years longer. The pension company will add seven years to the age difference so Linda is considered 17 years younger than the Richard. When they're calculating the benefit, this will be taken into account and the income will be significantly less. I would advise any couple in that situation to check out a life insurance policy instead. They might be further ahead in income even after paying the insurance premiums. (If Linda is 17 years older than Richard, first of all, you go girl! Second, the joint and last survivor benefit makes sense.)

A GIFT FROM CANADA CUSTOMS AND REVENUE AGENCY

If you're not already receiving a company pension plan or superannuation between age 65 and 69, the government has a nice little gift for you. For each of those five years, you are allowed $1,000 of pension income tax-free. CPP and OAS don't qualify for this deduction. To get it, you have to transfer some of your RRSP money into an RRIF or an annuity so that the money comes to you as income. People sometimes miss this opportunity when they're concerned about saving tax and may have enough income from other sources; they leave all their money in their RRSPs until they're 69. In doing so, they're missing the opportunity to receive $5,000 from their RRSP totally tax-free.

Age 69 And Over

You know you're really a senior when . . .

December 31 of your sixty-ninth year on the planet is the last day you can contribute to your RRSP, because after that your RRSP turns into a pumpkin. Most people are aware of that but some misunderstand what happens next. Even well-informed, reasonably sophisticated investors ask me if at age 69 the government will force them to take all their money out of their RRSPs and pay tax on it. No. The government will not make you pay tax on the full amount of your RRSP. However . . .

This is the deal. You *must* start taking income from your RRSP when you reach 69. You've never paid any tax on this money, so now the government wants to force you to start taking money out and paying tax on it. If you don't start taking income . . .*then* they'll tax the whole thing as one big chunk of money and you'll lose about half of the worth of your accumulated savings. You do not want to blast a big hole in the money you've slaved for and saved and invested over all these years.

You have two options. You can transfer your RRSP into a Registered Retirement Income Fund (RRIF) or you can transfer it into an annuity. At any time you can go from a RRIF to an annuity, but you can never convert an annuity back to a RRIF.

REGISTERED RETIREMENT INCOME FUND

A RRIF (pronounced *riff*) looks, walks and talks like an RRSP. The two differences are that you can no longer contribute to it and the government is forcing you to take a minimum percentage out and pay tax on it every year. The percentage you must take out goes up with your age. You can also remove money from a RRIF in lump sums as you need them (which may even push you up into the next tax bracket).

All the investments in your RRSP can be directly transferred to a RRIF: stocks, bonds, term deposits, business interests, real estate—whatever you've been investing in under the umbrella of your RRSP. But this transfer isn't going to just happen. You have to go and talk to someone and sign papers to make it so. The people who can do this are banks, trust companies, stockbrokers, life insurance agents, financial advisors, mutual fund salespeople, or people from the institution where you happen to have your RRSP. If you don't do this, as I said it before, *the government will deregister your RRSP and you will have pay tax as if the whole thing was your income for that year.*

This is a good opportunity to look at consolidating all your investments with one advisor or financial company so that you have one or two RRIFs instead of several. You can keep your diversified portfolio, but just move your investments under the same umbrella. As you grow older, you'll appreciate the simplicity.

Some people have enough income from other sources, and the income from a RRIF will increase their taxes, so they would prefer to take as little of that as possible. There is a slight break available here if you have a younger spouse. Although you have to take income once you reach 69, and the percentage of income you must take increases as you age, if your spouse is younger than you, you are allowed to base your calculations on the younger person's age. That means you will be able to take out a lower percentage and pay less tax.

ANNUITIES

Your other choice with your RRSP funds is to purchase a life annuity. This means that you liquidate some of your portfolio and hand it over to a life insurance company. The company will then guarantee you a set income for life. Whatever terms and conditions you've agreed to are fixed for life and the income is guaranteed until you die. The income is taxed as you receive it.

The RRIF has a lot more flexibility than the annuity, in that you can keep it in any kind of investment you had in your RRSP and it allows lump-sum withdrawals. But if you're a Spender, Builder or a Giver, you may take too many lump sums out of your RRIF and end up with no income. An annuity gives you income for the rest of your life, guaranteed until you die.

You can transfer any portion of your RRSP or RRIF into a life annuity. Generally if you have a partner and interest rates are low, a RRIF is the first step. However if your spouse dies or you are single, you need to have a good hard look at an annuity. If you have a substantial company pension plan or superannuation that will pay all your fixed expenses even if you require home care or need to go into long-term care, you may not need to look at an annuity at all. Otherwise an annuity has some significant advantages.

Being locked in is an annuity's single biggest plus, especially for people who are single for whatever reason. If you have no spouse or children, you are considered defenseless and a target to be ripped off. As hateful as it seems, there's a whole miserable element out there who prey on those they assume will be sweet, sympathetic, trusting or maybe a little confused—*i.e.*, seniors. These criminals are after big chunks of money, so if you depend on a monthly income to live on, they're less likely to get you to go to the bank and write a cheque for $100,000 to the bank inspector for the Republic of AgaWooga who needs to use your bank account to capture a serial forger named the Desert Cat.

One woman I know was a victim in a string of home repair rip-offs. The guy, who six months earlier had been charged with the same crime, went around to seniors and offered to do home repairs. He did a small repair on her siding and when she saw the bill she simply thought, oh my, haven't prices gone up. For about a $40 job, he charged $1,940. He even wrote out the cheque and had her sign it, as well as a contract that she didn't know she was signing. In this case it was fortunate that she lived in a small community and had some people watching over her. When she mentioned it to her gardener, he helped her take the case to court and get the money back. The gentleman had made her sign a contract, otherwise he would have gone to jail. As it was, the judge made him give back the whole amount, including the $40.

It's not just criminals either. Sometimes children don't always do the best thing by their parents. The kids use Mom's money to buy a bigger house so they can have Mom move into the suite they built for her. The intentions are really good. But after a while, it gets to be a bit of a burden to take care of Mom, so she goes to a retirement home and it's sort of forgotten that it was Mom's money that bought the house in the first place.

It's not meant in a bad way, but it just happens. Mom might have had plenty of money to take care of herself, but she allowed herself to become dependent on the children.

Then there's the Shopping Channel, which can become a real addiction for bored or lonely seniors. And often they don't even remember they've bought something so they buy another one. An annuity at least guarantees that they can't blow all their savings on George Foreman Electric Grills.

If you're single or your spouse has passed on, buy an annuity so you have a guaranteed income that will always provide for you to be in good long-term care or have good home care. That way the money will never disappear.

HOW TO BUY AN ANNUITY

Annuities are a challenge to buy because the rates vary so much from one source to another that you have to do a wide-ranging search, but at the same time the rates are only guaranteed for one day, two at the most. So when the time comes to buy one, you'll have to make a quick decision.

When you buy an annuity, you pay a certain amount of money and the company you buy it from pays you a set rate of interest on that money. These annuity rates are set by life insurance companies looking for cash for their own investments, therefore the field is very competitive. There can be big discrepancies between the lowest and highest rates offered. I ran a sample for one client looking to buy an $80,000 annuity. There was a $100-a-month range between the first and the fourteenth company—$100-a-month, $1,200-a-year—that can mean a lot. And that was on the measly sum of $80,000.

When you're ready to purchase an annuity, you need someone experienced who will shop the entire market for you. I suggest that you and your advisor do a couple of dry runs three to six months before you have to buy. That way you can see the wide range of returns. Make sure that your advisor is doing a total market search on your behalf so you know exactly what's out there.

A few practice runs will also enable you to feel fairly confident when the time comes to make that quick decision. The kinds of choices you make on your annuity will probably be the same ones you would make on a company pension plan. When you're thinking of buying annuities, you'll ask the same questions including:

- Do I want this to last until my death?
- Do I want it to go to my spouse after my death?
- If both of us die before our time, do we want it to go to our children (and receive less income now)?
- How long do we want it to last after we die?

You can add a guarantee for your estate if you wish. For example, a life annuity, guaranteed 10 years, means that you will receive an income for the rest of your life, but if you die two years into the annuity, your estate will receive the income for the balance of the 10 guaranteed years. That way your estate will not lose the value of the money that went to buy the annuity. If you are concerned about inflation, annuities can be calculated to grow with inflation, but you will pay more for them. If you've already considered all these variables, you'll be able to take advantage of the best annuity rates when they come up.

IMPAIRED ANNUITY

Any serious health problems in the past may qualify you for an impaired annuity which yields a higher return than a regular annuity. You're not usually asked about your health when you buy an annuity, so if you have or have had high blood pressure, a heart attack, cancer or another serious condition, be sure to bring it up when you're buying.

RRIF OR ANNUITY?

How do you choose between a RRIF, an annuity or a combination of the two? If interest rates are low, if you purchase a life annuity, the interest rate on that annuity will be fixed for life at that low rate. On the other hand, in the early eighties, many of my clients purchased life annuities at 18% interest, and these people are still receiving an 18% return on their money for life. Pretty happy folks.

In the event that both you and your spouse are very healthy, if interest rates are relatively low and you see inflation in the near future, you may choose to leave your investments as they were and just take the income you require from your RRIF. If your spouse dies, you need to reassess your whole financial picture. At that point, unless you have a guaranteed monthly pension that will cover all your needs, you will probably want to convert some of your money into an annuity to guarantee you a monthly income.

Extreme Spenders, Givers and Builders who can't handle the temptation of a big sum of money benefit from annuities because they can have a steady source of income with no possibility of getting at the capital.

I have noticed that as people get into their late seventies and early eighties, they like to simplify things. Too many choices become too much bother. An annuity, even if it's just enough to provide a decent monthly income, gives them peace of mind because it is guaranteed. Figure 11.1 outlines some of the major differences between RRIFs and annuities.

Differences Between a
Figure 11.1: RRIF and an Annuity

RRIF	Annuity
• monthly income as long as it lasts • lump sum available • can convert all or part to an annuity • rate of return variable • can make investment decisions • will pass on to estate	• guaranteed monthly income for life • no lump sum available • cannot convert to a RRIF • rate of return fixed • investment decisions made by financial institution • won't pass on to estate unless arrangements made

SHOULD I GET A REVERSE MORTGAGE?

When you bought your home, you paid the money owed on your mortgage to a financial institution while you lived in the house. With a reverse mortgage, the financial institution pays you a lump sum equal to a small percentage of the value of the house while you continue to live there. The money you receive is tax-free because it's capital on your principal residence.

When the house is sold, or if you repay the loan, the financial institution receives the initial amount along with compound interest. You won't be forced out of the home even if you outlive the value of the reverse mortgage. A lot of seniors who have no family are house-poor. They never want to leave their home if they don't have to (often my clients say they'll have to be carried out). They're not concerned with leaving an estate.

These are the people who are most interested in reverse mortgages, and for them this arrangement might make sense.

If a reverse mortgage means the difference between staying in your home and having to sell it, this may be an option for you, but I generally recommend these only as a last resort. Psychologically, a reverse mortgage can be very difficult: you've been conditioned your whole life to pay off the mortgage and be debt free and you're now doing the opposite. It also means that the entire value of the house won't go to the kids and grandkids, but then, they didn't work and struggle to buy that house in the first place. You did. If you need to go into a nursing home at some point, you can sell the house, pay off the reverse mortgage and still have enough left for care. Do some projections to see how much you will owe with the interest if you sell the house in five years.

Reverse mortgages can have very convoluted rules, and the companies that sell them require that you get independent legal advice before you buy one. Check it out with your financial advisor too—there may be other ways to stay in your house.

POWER OF ATTORNEY

There might come a time when you no longer have the ability to handle your own finances, either physically or mentally. Something as simple as not being able to sign your name could create serious complications in your financial dealings—and something that affects your brain could render you incapable of making decisions. Before anything like that happens, you should designate someone you trust to pay your bills and manage your money in the event that you become incapacitated, because you can't pass this on automatically. Just because you jointly own property with someone, that person may not be able to proceed on any kind of financial transaction without your signature. If you're not in a position to provide it and haven't designated anyone, the provincial government will select someone for you.

Power of attorney doesn't have to rest with an actual attorney; it just has to be someone who's competent to take care of your financial affairs, temporarily or permanently. The position can mean as little as doing your banking for you or as much as running your entire financial life. Your husband or wife, an adult child, another trusted family member, your lawyer, accountant, or financial planner can act as your power of attorney. The main criterion is that it be someone with your interests at heart.

Easier said than done, of course. How many people have been duped by someone they trusted completely? You can put limits on the power of attorney by stating, for instance, that it can't be used for buying and selling stocks, bonds or properties, or by declaring that a third party must be consulted on any transaction over a certain amount. You might prefer to choose two people: one who's good with finances and one who knows you and your wishes well and has no designs on your money. They will have joint power of attorney and will have to agree on any financial decisions.

You should also appoint someone in reserve in case the original person can't do it anymore; and you should choose this person with as much care as you did the first one (or two, or three).

To designate power of attorney you need to see a lawyer or a notary public.

WHAT TO DO WITH THE EXTRA

You've worked hard, saved carefully and invested well. Now you're enjoying a comfortable retirement with some to spare. What a wonderful thing, to be able to share your wealth. It doesn't even have to be a lot. Twenty or 30 dollars a month can build up into a very nice contribution to someone else's well-being.

You could leave it all in your will, but if you want to ensure that your family or your cause gets as much as possible, you're better off to start giving it away now. Here are ways you can give without causing a big tax burden to the recipient or yourself.

Giving to People

If you have substantially more than you need to support yourself, you and your beneficiaries can save tax if you simply give it to them while you're alive. A warning, though: don't give things away too soon. You don't want to empty your house of its contents while you're still living in it, and you don't want to give away so much of your money that you don't have the resources to do what you want (or need) to do. Be sure that you're taking care of yourself first, and you're prepared for any contingencies regarding your health.

Anyone can be given any amount of money and not pay tax on it. There's no limit. There's no paperwork. So if I give my daughter and son-in-law $5,000 or even $50,000, they don't have to add it to their income and be taxed on it. On top of that, I get to see them enjoying the money. All of this assumes, of course, that I've already paid tax on the original money and the interest or capital gains.

If money or family treasures pass to your beneficiaries in your will, the beneficiaries will then have to pay tax on some of the value. Giving money or possessions now to the people you want to have them could avert any misunderstandings or resentments later on when they have to figure out among themselves exactly what you meant when you said "You'll all get what you deserve." (If you would rather put these possessions in your will, the next chapter has guidelines on how to do it properly.)

Giving to Institutions

You can get a tax deduction by giving money, stocks, bonds, art, antiques, jewelry, collectibles, property or other items to a registered charity. This isn't always easy to do: your local museum may not have any room left (and would probably prefer a big undesignated cash donation instead). But if you succeed in donating your collection of Canadian art to some worthy institution, the institution gets the art and you get the tax write-off for what the art is worth.

When you give money or possessions to charity instead of willing them, the value of those possessions won't be added to your estate, which will cut down on the capital gains taxes and probate fees.

RESPs

If you contribute to your grandkids' RESPs, not only are you making it possible for them to have the education they deserve, you're sheltering the growth on your contribution from tax until they use it. The RESP can also earn a grant of up to $400 extra per year from the government, depending on how much you contribute. As a bonus, your own children, freed from the need to contribute to their children's RESPs, will be able to concentrate on saving for their own retirement, paying off the mortgage or maybe even working less and spending more time with their kids. RESP contributions are a gift that will last long beyond any other.

Life Insurance

Even if you only have a few dollars a month beyond what you need to live on, you can make an impressive contribution to your family or a charity, or even to your own estate to help with final taxes and expenses. It won't happen until after you're gone, but it will happen. The death benefit on a life insurance policy goes tax free to the named beneficiary on the policy. If you take out a whole life or universal life insurance policy, even for just $20 or $30 a month, your beneficiary will receive the death benefit tax free. Your benefit might work out to be several thousand dollars more than you paid for it . . . and did I mention it's all tax free?

You can also donate a life insurance policy to charity. You can give it to them now and deduct the life insurance premiums from your income tax. Or you can leave it to them in your will and the full amount of the life insurance policy is deductible by your estate. You can't do both, but either way, your money is working the way you want it to.

If you're so well off that you don't need life insurance, then life insurance is probably the best way to make sure your money goes to the people and organizations you want it to, and not to the government.

Foundations

A foundation enables someone with a significant amount of money (generally over $10,000) to give a specified amount away. It will usually be a capital endowment of a certain amount, and the earnings can be dispersed every year to your designated charities or to people who have applied for grants, or at the discretion of the people who run the foundation. If you don't have $10,000, many foundations allow you to set up an endowment fund to which you can contribute at least $1,000 every year until you have built up the required amount. Then the return from your endowment fund can be donated to the charity of your choosing.

Your endowment will continue long after you're gone, so it needs to be well thought out. Suppose, for instance, you set up your foundation to help diabetes research. As I write this, research is going well and it's improving the lives of people with diabetes every year. But what happens if somebody discovers a cure—a simple injection that will make every diabetic better? Suddenly there's no need for further research into diet planning or painless ways to get blood samples or blindness prevention. It's fixed! Now we have one dead-duck foundation. It can't help diabetes anymore, but that's all it's set up to do, and the terms of its mandate won't let it do anything else.

A foundation has to have the discretion to change mandates if change is needed. Set it up so that you, and later your estate, can decide where the money should go. If a cause ceases to be a cause, what's the next one?

There are two major benefits to setting up a foundation while you're alive. The first is an immediate tax deduction. The second is the joy of seeing the difference you're making in people's lives.

SAVING TAX IN RETIREMENT

Overall, remember the following points as you enjoy your retirement in order to minimize your taxes:

- Remember to roll your RRSP into a RRIF and/or purchase an annuity by December 31 of the year you turn 69.
- Continue paying into your RRSP until December 31 of the year you turn 69 so that you can get that tax year's refund.
- Continue paying into your younger spouse's RRSP and claiming the amount on your income tax.
- Base your minimum RRIF withdrawal on your younger spouse's age if you don't need the income.
- Use non-registered savings for big-ticket items instead of with-drawing large lump sums from your RRIF.
- Split CPP income with a spouse who earns less.
- Take similar incomes rather than one high and one low income.
- Take advantage of some cities' policy of deferring property taxes for seniors if you don't mind that the taxes will eventually come out of your estate.

And now, one last thing, although by no means the last thing you should think about. Estate planning is something that you do through-out your life. I only put it last, in the next chapter, because it scares so many people silly.

CHAPTER

ESTATE PLANNING

There are no luggage racks on a hearse. — Mom

"Oh boy, I'm going to spend several hours thinking about what happens when I'm dead. Whoopee." Okay, so this is several degrees of fun below winning the lottery. After all, *you* won't care if you die intestate. So just consider estate planning a chore that you really ought to get done.

And remember, just because you write a will doesn't mean that you're going to die right away. Nobody comes out and says it, but so many people come to me without prepared wills that I know this is one of their nagging fears. If anything, you'll be tempting fate more if you don't write a will. And yet making excuses is so much easier than actually doing it. As always, your financial attitude colours your specific reasoning:

- Spenders figure there won't be anything left anyway.
- Savers can't spend it themselves, but they don't want anyone else to get it.
- Builders think that they can go on building indefinitely and don't want to tie up any money.
- Givers want to take care of everybody now, but neglect to think about what happens when they're not here to help anymore.

No matter what your excuses are, you'll leave a nasty, expensive vortex in your wake if you don't make your wishes clear. Is that what you want?

Do you love someone? Do you want your money to accomplish something when you're gone? Do you just hate the thought of Canada Customs and Revenue Agency (CCRA) getting their fangs into your assets? Well make out a will, for heaven's sake! No matter how young you are. If you've gone through the exercises in Part One, you already have the information you need to plan your estate. If you haven't, you can embark on those exercises knowing that you'll be getting double the value: finding your Enough number *and* taking care of your will, all rolled into one. (Hmm. It's hard to make those things sound like a big thrill. But if you get them done, one tiny little nagging gremlin will be off your back. You'll feel better—maybe lots better.)

There are a lot of decisions involved in making a will, and it's best not to leave them until the day before you get on a transatlantic flight with your new spouse who never really cared for your kids and hates your ex and your sister and brother.

WHAT HAPPENS IF I DON'T HAVE A WILL?

If you die without specifying what you want to happen to your assets, you are causing a whole heap of trouble for the people who might otherwise have benefitted from them.

Probate

A person who dies leaves behind property, money and investments that no longer belong to anybody. Almost anything left behind has to be probated, which means the court has to establish what it's worth and give instructions for its disposition. Making a will does not entirely free your estate from probate fees, but not making a will ensures that your estate will have to pay them. That means a lawyer you don't know will be charging a percentage of all your money and possessions in order to distribute them to people you may not want to have them. On top of that, everything you owned is frozen until the probate is complete.

Capital Gains Tax

We don't have inheritance taxes in Canada, but we do have capital gains taxes. The difference between what you paid for your assets and what they're worth on the date of your death is calculated and the whole process is referred to as deemed disposition. Immediately, the probate process figures out what your estate owes in capital gains and also levies a probate fee. (They're called fees, but actually they're another form of tax because they're calculated as a percentage of the estate. This is how the provincial government gets its bite out of you.) If your spouse survives

HOW ROY INADVERTENTLY CUT FRANCES OUT

Roy and Frances live together and he supports her son from a previous marriage. If Roy dies without leaving a will, his bank accounts are frozen, any salary or pension still coming to him is frozen and none of his possessions can be sold until probate is complete. Frances isn't considered Roy's spouse in most provinces, and they don't own anything jointly, so she's out in the cold until then. Even after the estate is probated, she might not end up with as much as Roy would have liked her to have because most of his estate will automatically go to his blood relatives. If an old business partner, ex-wife or other creditor has a claim on the estate, whatever is necessary goes there. Roy and Frances may have been blissful together when he was alive, but when he sticks her with all that mess, even the memory of their love won't keep Frances going.

you, the taxes on the assets will be deferred until his or her death. If not, then all your assets are deemed to be sold on the day of your death and all taxes are due immediately. Sometimes CCRA will allow up to six months to pay, but that's not a long time.

What do the words "estate sale" mean to you? Bargain prices, right? If you haven't planned properly, your estate is held to ransom to pay the taxes. Those left behind might have to liquidate assets, sell the house or go through other major disruptions. So a little planning in this area goes a long, long way.

Family

Not making a will can cause incredible family strife, as in "Mom always said I'd get that." "Well she told me just before she died that it was mine." It's your stuff. Decide who's to get it and make sure your wishes are carried out by writing it in your will. Even the nicest families can be shredded by the ill feelings caused by unclear instructions. You need to bring this up with those you've chosen as your beneficiaries while you're still healthy and alert. They will object, saying they don't want to think about it, or they don't want you to think that all they care about is getting your things. Tell them that you don't plan on dying this minute, but you just want to get everything straightened out in case anything happens. Tell them what the will says and discuss the disposal of things like furniture, art and other household effects. Ask them what they want, and once they have chosen, put it in writing and make sure they agree that you've got it right. Often sentiment plays as much a part in people's choices as value, so never underestimate how tenacious people can be when they're going after something with sentimental value.

LAYING THE GROUNDWORK

A will is a legal document in which you say what you want to happen to your money and property. At its most basic, it's what is called a holograph, a handwritten statement witnessed by two people who are not named in the will. This is legal only in some provinces.

At its best, a will is prepared with the help of a lawyer or notary public, so it gives clear directions that aren't open to misinterpretation or legal challenge. If you want someone—your children, spouse, parents, other dependants, preferred charities—to get as much of your money as possible, you have to make sure that your wishes are carried out with the smallest tax penalty possible.

You can start the preparations for a will on your own. There are books and software programs available to help you, and notaries public usually have free forms where you can list your assets and make decisions about what to do with them. These resources are excellent for helping you do the groundwork. Your financial planner, accountant, life insurance professional, pension plan consultant and banker can also point out ways in which your estate can save tax and probate fees. Then, when it comes time to prepare the final document, I urge you to use the guidance of a lawyer or a notary public. The money you'll pay now can save your estate hundreds or thousands of dollars later.

To make it easier on you, I'll list the basic things you have to think about when you're preparing a will.

Who Will Raise My Children?

What will happen to your children? This conundrum is the main reason people fail to make out their wills. If there's no will, the court will appoint a guardian and you, being dead, will have no say in who is chosen. Surely you at least want to make sure that your kids will be raised by Ward and June Cleaver rather than Dr. Evil.

Of course there's nobody good enough to take over the rearing of your children. Or the people you'd like to take over the job won't, or can't.

Eliminate that thought immediately. This is a terrible responsibility to burden your friends or relatives with. But if you don't designate guardians for your kids, the job will automatically go to your parents or your spouse's parents, if they're still alive. But they may no longer have the energy or inclination to raise children.

This is a tough one, but once you find people you respect who agree to love and care for your children if you're no longer around, the rest is easier. By the way, don't spring this on someone. How would you feel if one day you woke up and discovered you had two more kids in your household?

You might consider setting up joint custodianship. Say you have one person who's wonderful with kids and another who's wonderful with money—which do you choose? You can have both, each serving a different role. The financial person can be the executor of your will and can have discretion over how to best fulfill your wishes in dispersing the money. That could include giving the guardians access to capital as well as interest if they need it to provide for the kids.

In the case of divided families, everything becomes much more emotional and tied up in legalities. I won't say a word about these cases because each one is complicated in its own special way. The only thing I will say is, first: make a will. Second: make a will after you've consulted with a financial advisor and a lawyer or notary public.

How Do I Make Sure My Kids are Taken Care of?

If your dependants include young kids or adult children with disabilities that will make it difficult for them to take care of themselves, set up a trust on your death that will either handle the money until they are older, or take care of them for life. A trust can distribute income on the capital or it can eventually distribute the capital itself.

If you have children, I urge you to do this. It's the only way to make absolutely sure that your children will be taken care of.

One major recommendation is that you treat all your children equally, even if some have done better than others and don't seem to need anything. There are a few big exceptions: if you've already given substantial gifts to one child and not the others, those gifts can also be equalled out in the will. A child who has spent a great deal more time and energy taking care of you than the other siblings, a child who's involved in the family business, or a child with special needs—in those cases the rest of the family will (or should) understand if that sibling receives more.

Francine's Worst Case Scenario

Early in my career I would have thought that any spouse would take care of the kids, but one sad incident changed my mind. I was still in my twenties when I dealt with Francine, a lovely young woman with two children from a previous marriage and one from her current marriage. When we were talking about her life insurance I suggested that she leave the death benefit proceeds in trust for the kids, but she said no, she believed that her wonderful husband would take care of them forever. The first clue was that he didn't want her to buy the policy in the first place—didn't believe in them—and he made her pay for it out of her money. She named him the beneficiary, assuming that if she died, he would naturally take care of all of three kids identically. Well, in a way, he did. Francine did die, and he took all the money, left all three of the kids with his sister-in-law, and nobody's heard much from him since. His wife was not a stupid woman: it's just that no one can predict how someone, even a loved one, will react under pressure.

When that happened I was ready to quit financial planning. Here I'd had a chance to help this woman and her children and I'd been no help at all. I'd suggested, but I hadn't insisted. But I stayed in the business, and since that time I have used that true story to persuade hundreds of people to stipulate in their will that a trust will be set up for their minor children, never to be needed, we hope.

Special needs, by the way, don't include criminal tendencies, an inability to keep a job, a drug habit or expensive and unaffordable tastes. Parents have a tendency to help the wounded bird, and all that does is keep the bird wounded. The message to the other kids is that you love the wounded one more, and when Mom and Dad die, the others are certainly not going to take up the slack. If I've learned one thing in my years as a financial advisor it's that people who never have to take responsibility for themselves never will. It's too easy to depend on someone else's largesse.

If you do plan to treat the children unequally or if you want a great deal of your estate to go to charity, you should inform the children of the decision and discuss why. This will alleviate disputes among your children after you're gone because they'll know exactly what your intentions were and what was going on in your head when you made them. The kids can be mad at the parents but not mad at each other, and not suspicious that there was some wheeling and dealing undertaken by the other siblings to get the good stuff.

When you write your will, let your children know that you love them equally by distributing your after-tax gifts among them equally.

How Do I Make Sure My Spouse is Taken Care of?

Spouses don't pay any tax on the estate until the last survivor dies. Everything you own jointly automatically belongs to your spouse with no probate required and no capital gains payable. Still, if you want to make absolutely sure, leave a will, especially if you have some separate property that you want to remain separate.

Make sure it's an up-to-date will, too. If you wrote a will when you were married to someone else, change it so that your current spouse is your beneficiary. Otherwise . . . deep trouble. Update your will whenever you go through a major life change: if you marry, divorce, remarry or are widowed; have a child, adopt a child, become a step-parent or lose a child; start a business or wrap one up. Contact your lawyer or notary public and find out what it will take to bring your will in step with your life now.

Specify that your home goes to your spouse, if you're not already joint owners. Make sure your spouse does the same for you too, especially if the house is in only one name. One couple I knew arranged their wills on the assumption that he would die first. The house was in her name anyway, and she left it to the children. But she died first, and the kids sold "their" house from under their father! He could have gone to court and demanded his right to half the house because it was his principal residence, but he was too devastated that his children could turn on him like that. His only meagre consolation was that three years after they'd sold the house, it had doubled in value. (I still have trouble believing that children would do that to a parent, but then again, he and his wife had both been Givers who were always helping the kids out when they got into trouble. The kids eventually came to believe that whatever they wanted or thought they needed would be automatically granted. I wage a constant battle against parents who won't let their kids make mistakes or dig themselves out of the troubles they have created for themselves.)

You can also designate your spouse as the beneficiary of your RRSP or RRIF. Those will simply roll over into your spouse's RRSP or RRIF tax-free—for now. Your spouse's estate will eventually have to pay the income tax on what's left.

Life insurance passes to the beneficiary tax free, so it is particularly helpful for covering your final taxes and expenses. If you calculate the amount of tax that your estate will have to pay, then take out a life insurance policy for that amount. Your family won't have to liquidate any investments in order to pay capital gains and probate fees.

Another advantage of life insurance is that it is confidential, whereas your will is a matter of public record. If you have some business interests that someone might come after, you can buy life insurance to make sure that your spouse and children will have enough to support them. They won't have to pay tax on the proceeds and no one with an interest in your estate need know about the money.

If you don't think your mate manages money well, you might want to consider a spousal trust. That will allow you to specify a certain monthly income for your widow or widower that cannot be transferred or willed to anyone else. That way, no matter how irresponsible your spouse is, you can make sure that your children will eventually get some of your estate. You can also make sure that any future wives or husbands won't be able to get their hands on it. Your lawyer or planner can see if this option is right for you.

What Happens to the House?

Your family home—primary residence in legal terms—will pass to anyone you choose tax free. Only probate fees will be charged on the inheritance.

Other properties, like the beach cottage, revenue property or the *pied-à-terre* in the big city are subject to capital gains tax. I'm often asked "Can I just add my children's names to these properties?" You can, but the moment you do, the properties are deemed to be sold and you will have to pay capital gains on the difference. So if you bought your summer cabin 40 years ago for $10,000 and it's now worth half a million, you have a $490,000 capital gain. If there's been virtually no change in the value, then you can add another name without tax consequences: then the only issue is giving up control.

Before you arrange joint ownership with anyone, remember that they will now have as much say in what happens to the property as you will. If your co-owner is not cooperative, there could be trouble.

Family properties with a lot of happy memories attached to them can become huge burdens when the parents are gone and the siblings and their families have to work out deals for equitable sharing. Often one element will want to sell and another will want to keep the property in the family for posterity. These issues can blow families apart. Maybe you can defuse the whole situation by making a decision before someone else has to. If only one child wants to keep the cottage and the other two would rather sell it, you could leave it to the one who wants it and leave the others something else of equal value. Don't forget to calculate the capital gains each child will have to pay so that one child isn't getting saddled with a huge tax bill while others get off scot-free. It's not just the value of the property you're bequeathing, it's the taxes too.

WHAT HAPPENS TO MY RRSP?

When you're leaving everything to your spouse, it's very simple. Just designate your spouse as your beneficiary and it will roll over without any tax consequences.

Leave it to anyone else and they will have to pay income tax on it. If you want to divide your estate equally, you may be tempted to take that into consideration when you're deciding how much each person gets, but there's a fly in this ointment. Say you want to leave equal amounts to your sister Janet and your brother Robert. Knowing that Janet will have to pay income tax on the $100,000 RRSP you're leaving her, you leave Robert your non-registered savings of $50,000, on which he won't have to pay income tax. That should work out about even, right? No, and here's why. Any taxes on your estate will come out of the non-registered money. Robert will have to pay your final income tax as well as probate out of his $50,000. He could end up with nothing, while Janet gets whatever's left from the RRSP after she's paid income tax. Because of issues like these, it's worth checking with your accountant, lawyer or financial advisor when you're making a will.

HOW DO I CHOOSE MY EXECUTOR?

Being an executor is a lot of work, especially for someone who never expected to be saddled with the job, so the person you designate as your executor might not see it as a great compliment. The executor's job is to make sure any debts are paid out of the estate, then carry out the terms of your will with what's left over (charmingly called the "residue"). If the will is clear and unassailable, the job is a great deal easier. I know one person, the ex-wife of the deceased, who had no idea she'd been appointed until the lawyer who read the will informed her. At that point, she was designated to carry out the terms of a will that specified that "my estate should be distributed among any of my friends who need help." After months of long-distance phone calling and cross-checking to see who his friends were and which of them were in a bad state, she couldn't help thinking that he was getting back at her.

It's a good idea to appoint as your executor someone who has some experience dealing with finances, because taxes, debts and probate can get very tricky. You should also assign some form of payment, because this person will be doing a lot of work on your behalf.

HOW TO SAVE TAX AND PROBATE ON YOUR ESTATE

Keep these points in mind as you plan your estate:

- Plan your will and make it legal.
- Don't worry about your principal residence: it passes tax free to any designated beneficiary, or to the other person who's living there.
- If you have a spouse 69 or younger, have your estate contribute to a spousal RRSP.
- Make sure you and your spouse jointly own everything you want to pass to each other.
- Invest in insurance policies that will provide income for your family.
- Consider buying joint last-to-die insurance to cover your final taxes.
- Designate the people you wish as beneficiaries of your insurance policies, pension and RRSPs.
- Diminish the value of your estate by giving money and possessions away while you're alive (although not too soon).
- Set up a foundation that will provide interest to designated causes. If you donate to charities, there will be tax deductions.
- Create trusts for those who are too young to inherit or who will need regular income.

Planning your estate is not the most fun you'll ever have (at least I sure hope not!) but once you've managed to organize it the first time, it's just a matter of keeping your will and financial affairs in order and up-to-date. This is something you do for others, and there is a good feeling that comes from that.

CHAPTER

TWENTY THOUGHTS TO HELP YOU STAY ON TRACK

If you've read this far, even if you haven't done any of the work yet, you have an idea of how to achieve financial peace of mind. *How Much Is Enough* was designed to motivate you by working with your individual needs and desires. But all of us humans sometimes have trouble focusing on the future when the present is gleaming and glittering right in front of us. So much to build, to spend, to give, and yes, even to save. If you go off track occasionally, don't beat yourself up. Just get back in there and keep at it. Here's a collection of thoughts that might help you keep at it when temptation strikes.

(And if you're just peeking at the back page, here's some free advice.)

- It's never too late to start financial planning (or too early).
- A little is better than nothing.
- Any interest you pay is money that you can't spend on yourself.
- Clearing up debt is short-term pain for long-term gain.
- Let compound interest work for you, not against you.
- Pay yourself first: take at least 10% off the top to save and invest.
- RRSPs put more money in your hands and RESPs put more money in your children's hands.
- Revisit your wish list to remember what you're aiming for.
- If you didn't want something in the first place, it's not a deal no matter how cheap it is.
- Never hand over financial control—no one else cares about your future the way you do.
- Invest only in things you understand and feel comfortable with.
- If you miss an opportunity, there will always be others.

- Get rich slowly—put your money regularly into solid investments.
- Markets go up and down. Don't panic.
- Borrow only for things that appreciate in value (except for your first car).
- A financial advisor can make sure you're making the most from your money.
- By taking care of yourself, you're helping other people.
- Reward yourself in big and little ways for staying on track.
- If you know what you want, you can get it.
- Keep track of where you are on the road to where you're going.

There's nothing like knowing that you're making choices because you want to, not because you have to. Some people never want to leave their doorstep. Some want to go to the ends of the earth. Some want all the toys. Some don't care if they have any. Some want to save the world. Some want to escape from it. Each of us takes a different road, but when you have Enough to take you there, isn't the journey wonderful?

APPENDIX

Financial planners go by many different names, and come from many different fields. Here are the names and Web site addresses of the various associations of financial planners. Each of them will have a list of members in your area, and should be able to tell you their areas of expertise apart from general financial planning.

Acronym	Name	Certified by	Web site
CFA	Chartered Financial Analyst	Assn for Investment Management & Research	**www.aimr.org**
CFP	Certified Financial Planner	Financial Planners Standards Council	**www.cfp-ca.org**
CHFC	Chartered Financial Consultant	Cdn Assn of Insurance & Financial Advisors	**www.caifa.com**
FMA	Financial Management Advisor	Canadian Securities Institute	**www.csi.ca**
PFP	Personal Financial Planner	Institute of Canadian Bankers	**www.icb.org**

INDEX

ABOUT THE AUTHOR

Diane McCurdy grew up in Winnipeg, the youngest in a family of ten children. At the age of twenty she started PR work in the life insurance business. In just over a year she was one of the first female salespeople in Winnipeg. Noticing that she wasn't being taken seriously by bankers, she enrolled in courses to learn more about finance and started her own business, buying, renovating and selling old houses. In 1976 she began her own insurance agency (while also moonlighting as a partner in an ice cream store). Her drive and energy made heads turn and she was profiled in *Chatelaine* the *Globe and Mail* and numerous other publications across the country.

From the start she called herself a financial planner—a little-used term at the time. She realized that in order to meet people's insurance needs, she had to look at their entire financial situation. After only three years as an agent, she qualified for the prestigious Million Dollar Round Table.

A warmer climate lured her to Vancouver in 1979 where she built a practice that continues to concentrate on offering full service with personal attention to her 1,100 clients.

Diane has spent two years on the planned giving committee for the largest individual charitable foundation in North America, the Vancouver Foundation, and six years on the committee doing the same work for Children's Hospital. She's also a great believer in mentoring and is guiding two young women in the financial planning business.

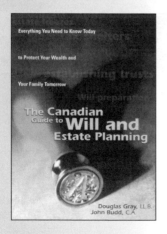
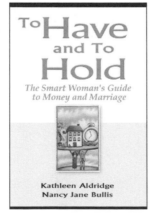
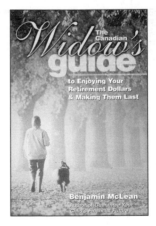